The Great Whales

In the last fifty years, two million whales have been killed.

The Great Whales

Faith McNulty

Illustrations by Richard Cuffari

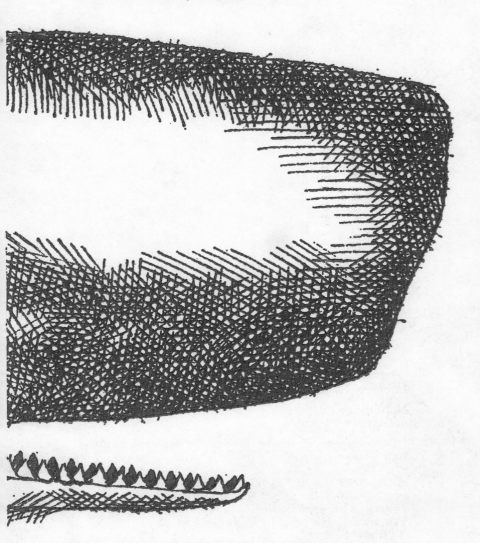

Doubleday & Company, Inc., Garden City, New York 1974

The contents of this book originally appeared in
The New Yorker © 1973, in slightly different form.

Library of Congress Cataloging in Publication Data

McNulty, Faith.
    The great whales.

"The contents of this book originally appeared in the
New Yorker . . . in slightly different form."
    1. Whales.   I.   Title.
QL737.c4м28   599′.51
ISBN 0-385-00297-1
Library of Congress Catalog Card Number 72–96270

By the same author

MUST THEY DIE?
The Strange Case of
the Prairie Dog
and the
Black-footed Ferret

THE WHOOPING CRANE

1798483

The Great Whales

O F all our fellow-mammals, the most remote and the most difficult to understand is the great whale. Its size and the alien element it inhabits cut it off from us both in imagination and as an object of study. It is more nearly possible to feel kinship with a mouse, and a mouse is also immeasurably easier for a scientist to observe. Men have pursued whales for centuries, and killed them with unbounded cruelty and in staggering numbers, without learning much more than the simplest facts about their anatomy and their habits. Most of our knowledge of whales, in fact, has been derived from dead whales. Their giant corpses have been dissected, and scientists have charted their astonishing insides: arteries with the circumference of stovepipes, hearts weighing a thousand pounds, and large, complex brains suggesting extraordinary mental powers. A mass of statistics records the location, the species, the size, the sex, and the reproductive state of virtually all the great whales killed over the last fifty years. If a female carried an unborn whale (and nearly half of the females killed have), sometimes it, too, has been measured before being shovelled into the cooking pots. From these data, cetologists have in recent years tried to figure out how many whales remain in the oceans and how many can be killed annually without destroying the various species for all time. Thus, while there is a large store of vital statistics on past generations of whales, long since converted into margarine and mink food, little is known of the living, breathing animals. This paradox exists partly because ce-

tologists, many of them tied to the whaling industry, have been forced to consider whales primarily
as a crop, but also because the great whales present
the field biologist with one of the most baffling
problems in nature. How do you study a living animal that is usually inaudible and is visible only in
glimpses? With all the difficulties, some interesting
items have been gathered just in the past few years.
The fact that the great whales make sounds underwater, for instance, is a recent discovery, and biologists are now puzzling over its meaning. Also, in
1971, for the first time, a great whale was kept in
captivity and carefully observed by scientists.

By now, most newspaper readers are aware that
the great whales have been hunted with such rapac-
ity and improvidence that there is fear that some
species may become extinct. The Japanese and the
Russians are currently doing the major share of the
killing. The British, the Norwegians, and the
Dutch, who were once among the principal killers
of whales, left the major hunting grounds—the
Antarctic and the North Pacific—a few years ago,
when the supply of whales fell so low that their expeditions became unprofitable. Though the United
States killed more than its share in the last century,
American whaling activities, which had been negligible for the previous forty years, ceased entirely
in 1971, so, for once, we needn't feel guilty about
an ecological outrage. On the other hand, we seem
to be helpless to do anything about this one. In
1970, conservationists persuaded Secretary of the
Interior Walter Hickel to put eight species of great

whales on the list of endangered animals whose products may not be imported into this country— a move that was strongly opposed by our Department of State, which would have preferred not to upset trade relations with Japan. The ban has undoubtedly had an important moral effect, but it has not diminished the killing of whales, because the whalers have found sufficient market for their products elsewhere. In 1971, the United States took another important step: both houses of Congress passed resolutions calling for a ten-year international moratorium on the commercial killing of whales and asking our State Department to negotiate to that end. Still other victories for the conservationists came in 1972, when Canada shut down shore stations from which whales were killed in the North Atlantic, and in 1973, when Britain banned the importation of all whale products except a few from sperm whales.

Whales, as prey, are prize packages, worth between ten and thirty thousand dollars apiece, which belong to no one. Whaling "expeditions" (of which the Japanese during the 1972–73 season had four and the Russians three in the Antarctic) each consist of a factory ship almost as big as an aircraft carrier, attended by a fleet of small, fast catcher boats that roam in search of whales. Each catcher kills whales at an average rate of one or two a day with the utmost efficiency. The whales are run down and then killed by harpoons, fired from cannons, which carry explosive charges that detonate inside the whales. The whales usually die within fifteen or twenty minutes, in gigantic, bloody flurries that churn the sea to red foam, but sometimes the death throes are more prolonged. (Humanitarians have pressed the whalers to devise less ghastly methods, but without success.) The catcher boat marks the corpse of a whale with a radio beacon so that it can be picked up by the factory ship while the catcher continues the hunt. When the factory ship arrives, huge winches haul the giant body of the dead whale up a ramp at the stern and onto a half acre of deck, where work gangs armed with flensing knives cut it into pieces. The bones and the blubber are boiled in great vats within the ship to extract the oil. The meat is frozen, some of it for human consumption (whale meat is eaten, though not in large quantities, by the Japanese and Russians), but much of it as food for dogs or ranch mink. In forty-five minutes, a whale eighty feet long and weighing a hundred tons can be converted into 96.66 long tons of raw material. Much whale oil is made into margarine, and that of sperm whales (which is inedible) makes an especially fine lubricant; all sorts of whale oil can be ingredients of cosmetics, shoe polish, paint, and soap. Whale products are used thus because they are the cheapest and most convenient raw material. In every case, a substitute can be found.

Though whales are diminishing in numbers, whaling goes on, partly because the equipment for it exists. Floating whale factories represent large investments of rubles and yen, and it is more profitable to use them even for a small catch than to scrap them. If the supply of large whales is finally exhausted, there will still be lesser species of Cetacea—pilot whales, beaked whales, and killer whales, for instance, and even the smaller dolphins —that can be exploited. The number of whales taken in modern whaling is huge. In the last fifty years, two million have been killed. The high point of the massacre was sixty-seven thousand, reached in 1962. Since then, the number has gone down drastically, but it is still very large. In the past three seasons the figure has averaged about thirty-seven thousand—a decline owing mainly to the fact there were fewer whales to be killed.

Theoretically, whaling is regulated by the International Whaling Commission, representing both the active whaling nations and nations with an interest in whaling, the United States among them. (Several countries, including Iceland, Norway, and South Africa, have no factory ships but use smaller vessels to kill whales migrating off their shores and tow them to shore stations for processing.) The commission was founded after the Second World War, with the laudable intent of restraining the excessive killing of whales. Unfortunately, the owners of whaling vessels (or, in the case of Russia, the officials governing the industry) have largely called the tune. In bargaining disguised as "conservation," the whaling nations have haggled over their share of the remaining whales, disputed scientific warnings that whales are dwindling, and piously agreed to stop killing endangered species only when there were so few individuals left that the commercial sacrifice was negligible.

At the first United Nations Conference on the Human Environment, held in Stockholm in June of last year, a proposal by the United States for a cease-fire on whales passed unanimously. Despite valiant efforts by Russell E. Train (chairman of the Council on Environmental Quality and spokesman in 1972 for the United States delegation to the I.W.C.), we have had less luck at recent meetings of the I.W.C., which rejected the same proposal in late June, 1972, and again this year. The arguments of Robert M. White, the commissioner of the United States delegation to the I.W.C. in 1973, were vehemently opposed by the Japanese delegation, consisting of the owners of the major Japanese whaling companies. Some reform of the rules under which the whaling fleets operate, which has been recommended by scientists for decades, has been grudgingly accepted by the commissioners, but the over-all quota, even though it has been lowered, is still set at a figure—thirty-seven thousand five hundred for the 1973–74 season—that appalls conservationists. The most signal achievement at the recent meeting was a ban on the hunting of fin whales in the Antarctic, but since it was voted over the objections of both Russia and Japan, nobody knows whether it will be observed. Furthermore, it is to be put into effect in phases over three years, and by its terms 1,450 fin whales may be killed in the Antarctic this coming season. The fin whale is the second-largest whale, and there were once something like half a million of these animals. A guess, possibly optimistic, puts their current number in the Antarctic at eighty thousand—still high enough to be tempting to the hunters.

In truth, the I.W.C., even if it means well (and apologists claim to see signs of reform), seems to be a toothless watchdog. Member nations are not bound to abide by its decisions; when the Russians and the Japanese are outvoted by more conservation-minded members, they are still free to enter a formal objection and do as they please. The main argument for the continued existence of the commission is that it provides a framework for negotiation, and that the agreements it has reached are better than nothing. Should the commission collapse, the Russians and the Japanese might decide to race each other for the last whales and finish things then and there. Most observers feel, however, that if whaling is to be stopped while there are still some whales left to save, the halt will come about as a result of conservationists' inspiring their governments to put heavy trade pressure on Russia and Japan, Scott McVay, of the Environmental Defense Fund, an American private conservation group that has been working for the past several years to influence world opinion to spare the whales, has made trips to both Japan and Russia. He feels that the Russians show more signs of willingness to slow down the hunt than do the Japanese. Most conservationists agree that the Japanese apparently intend to go on killing whales as long as possible—both out of an urge for profit and a national need for protein. Leaders of the conservation fight in this country talk of a United States boycott of Japanese goods and an appeal to the Common Market to close off Europe as a market for whale products. This would be a tall order, but these are days when environmental zeal is achieving what heretofore seemed impossible, and such tactics, which reduce the issue to dollars, rubles, and yen, are the only ones likely to work where appeals to humanity, ethics, and pure reason have failed.

WHEN I first became concerned with whales, I, like most people, had never seen a member of their order larger than a dolphin. In fact, I didn't know that there was any way to see a great whale short of shipping on a whaling vessel bound for the Antarctic. But the idea of seeing a whale, of trying to get some sense of the nature of this extraordinary beast, fascinated me, and when I learned that whales can easily be seen in several places close to our shores I decided to go to two of them and try to see some. The places I planned to visit were the waters off Bermuda, where humpback whales migrating northward congregate in early spring, and Scammon Lagoon, in Baja California, where the great gray whales come to mate and give birth. Off Bermuda, the songs of the humpbacks have been studied by Dr. Roger S. Payne, a biologist associated with Rockefeller University and the New York Zoological Society; Scammon Lagoon is visited by tourist expeditions

arranged by the Natural History Museum of San
Diego. Accordingly, I made arrangements to go to
Bermuda with Dr. Payne and later to make the trip
to Scammon. Meanwhile, I gathered some basic
information about whales.

As most of us have learned at some time, there
are two kinds—those with teeth and those with a
sievelike arrangement of baleen, or whalebone, in
their mouths which enables them to strain small organisms from the water. The baleen whales, of
which there are ten species, constitute the suborder
Mysticeti of the order Cetacea, and the toothed
whales constitute the suborder Odontoceti.
Toothed and baleen whales evolved separately
from different land animals, which took to the sea
independently of each other, and they are not believed to be closely related. The baleen whales are
the most "whalelike." They make up the large ma-
jority of the so-called great whales—the leviathans.
The blue whales, which may be a hundred feet
long and weigh more than a hundred tons, and all
the other huge whales except the sperm are baleen
whales. The toothed whales, familiarly represented
by the numerous kinds of dolphins and porpoises,
are mostly small, the only really large toothed species being the sperm whale. (Moby Dick was, of
course, a sperm whale.) Toothed whales make up a
large and varied group, which includes the beluga,
or white whale; the narwhal, which has a strange,
twisted tusk; the friendly little pilot whale; and the
killer whale, largest of the dolphins. Since both of
the species I expected to see—humpback and gray

—were baleen whales, I decided to concentrate more on this suborder.

Whales carry within them clear evidence of their origin on land. Fifty million years and more of life in the water has shaped and polished them like stones, gently rubbing away such externals as fur, outer ears, hind legs, and front toes, but the memory of all these things has not been quite erased from the genes. Whales no longer need a pelvis, but in the muscle tissue on either side of the genital opening is a small bone, only a foot long in the large whales, that is a relic of the pelvis they possessed when they were four-legged animals. The embryo whale is shaped very much like the embryo pig—or the embryo human being, for that matter —with a round head, a snout, a neck, ridges where ears might grow, and buds where hind legs should be. Usually, the vestigial hind legs disappear as the whale matures, but now and then the genes slip back an eon and legs are partially formed. Within the flipper are bones almost identical with those in human arms and hands. Most whales have five finger bones, though some lack a thumb. All the arm joints are rigid and buried within the flipper. Only the shoulders are workable.

Whales breathe through an aperture at or near the top of the head, the area closest to the surface of the water. Toothed whales have a single blowhole, and baleen whales have two. Embryos of either kind, however, have two nostrils at the tip of the snout, like any land animal; the nostrils migrate during foetal development. Every whale contains within its streamlined hide the usual liver and lights of a land animal. The whale's blood is warm, driven by its huge heart. It takes seven strong men to drag the six-foot heart of a blue whale across the deck of a whaling ship. Nevertheless, its proportion to the animal's body weight is the same as that of a chimpanzee's or a rabbit's. The cetacean stomach is compartmented and resembles that of a cow. The whale's reproductive system is quite standard for mammals except that the external sex organs have moved inside, recessed within a slit in the whale's belly, with the mammary glands in two smaller slits on either side. All adult whales have only two teats, but the embryo porpoise has eight, indicating that long ago its young arrived in litters. All cetaceans now have only one offspring at a time. Whales have lost their body hair entirely, but whiskers survive on the chin and tip of the upper jaw of baleen whales. These are evidently tactile organs, for they are richly surrounded with blood and nerves. Their number varies from fifty to two hundred and fifty in different species. The feeding arrangement of baleen whales is unique. In place of teeth there is, growing from the upper jaw, a comb-like structure of flat strips of whalebone, half an inch or so apart, ending in a coarse fringe. (Whalebone is not bone but a substance akin to hair or finger-nails.) When the baleen whale feeds, it simply engulfs a mouthful of water and whatever organisms the water contains; then, perhaps with the aid of its vast, cushiony tongue, it squirts the water out through the sieve of baleen and swallows whatever has been trapped and left behind. Differences in the embryos of toothed and baleen whales suggest that baleen whales are descended from short-tailed land animals and toothed whales from long-tailed land animals. The two suborders of whales resemble each other not because of common ancestry but because the demands of aquatic life have dictated similar adaptations. There is a fossil record of various kinds of primitive whales, known as Archaeoceti, which became extinct twenty-five million years ago. Some of them must have looked rather like sea serpents, but they possessed a pelvic girdle, forelegs that bent at the elbow, and nostrils halfway between the snout and the top of the head. Thus in form they were closer to their land-dwelling ancestors than are modern whales. The earliest fossils of baleen whales date from the mid-Oligocene, twenty-seven million years ago. These early whales were small—about the size of dolphins—and had teeth. The embryos of certain baleen whales still have tooth buds hidden in the gums; it is only in the last few million years that baleen whales have lost their teeth and evolved to their enormous size. Blood tests indicate that the nearest living relatives of both baleen and toothed whales are, somewhat surprisingly, the Artiodactyla—the ungulates with an even number of toes, such as cattle, sheep, camels, and hippopotamuses.

WHALES may once have walked into the sea on four legs, but they cannot be thought of as streamlined cows—or as air-breathing fish. They are unique in numerous ways, and difficult for the zoologist to classify. One taxonomist, G. G. Simpson, wrote: "Cetaceans are the most peculiar and aberrant of mammals. . . . There is no proper place for them in a scala naturae." Size, of course, is the whale's outstanding characteristic. Even a small whale is big by land standards. The size of land animals is limited by the ability of their legs to carry them, and this limit was reached by the prehistoric giant reptiles. Probably those reptiles were partly aquatic and regularly supported their bulk in the water of swamps. Whales, being totally waterborne, are not hampered by weight, but even in the sea there is a size limit beyond which organs cannot cope with physiological processes. Up to that point, great size is an advantage to a warm-blooded animal, since its foremost problem is how to keep warm. Water conducts heat twenty-seven times as rapidly as air, and the flow of water past a whale's skin robs it of heat just as a constant breeze would. The whale's great size is a defense against cold, and so is its streamlined shape, which reduces its surface and thus its contact with the water. There can be no small warm-blooded creatures in the sea—no sea mice or sea rabbits.

From the eternal chill of its world the whale has no hiding place. It cannot curl up or take shelter to keep warm, and so it has developed protective devices. It has a high metabolism—an internal heating plant operating at top draft—that allows it to move ceaselessly. (Whales are said to sleep mostly when they are in the warmer latitudes to which most of them move in winter.) The whale has an extraordinary layer of insulation—a coat of blubber that holds in heat like asbestos around a stove. There may be twenty tons of blubber on a ninety-foot blue whale, and the blubber of a Greenland whale may constitute almost half its weight, wrapping its internal organs in a layer two feet thick. This permanent insulation presents the whale with problems similar to those of a man with only one coat for all occasions. The whale cannot sweat or pant to cool off, so it would seem that, with exertion, it might fatally overheat. Cetologists believe that its fins, which are without blubber and have a rich blood supply, may act as devices to liberate excess heat. Fortunately for the whale, temperatures in the sea don't reach great extremes and don't fluctuate sharply. There is only a forty-five-degree difference between the waters of the tropics and the poles. The distribution of food also works out neatly to the baleen whale's advantage. It is plentiful in cold water, where it is most needed, and scarcer in warm water, where the whale can do without it.

The whale's great body is covered with a skin designed to aid its swift passage through the water. It is extremely thin and as smooth as glass. The only portion of the skin of most whales that is thick enough for use as leather is that of the penis, which whalers have been known to convert into golf bags. The whale's skin is often marked with scars where the whale has bumped into ice floes. The mouths of lampreys leave round scars on whales, and various small crustaceans attach themselves to them; a humpback has been known to carry a thousand pounds of barnacles. Killer whales attack and scar the large baleen whales.

The skeleton of the whale is designed not to bear weight but to anchor a giant musculature. There are forty tons of muscle in a hundred-ton blue whale, a great mass of it in the lower back to move the tail and its flukes. The bones are light and spongy, with a fatty marrow, which produces a great deal of oil when they are boiled by whalers. Stripped of flesh, the skeleton of a whale has a profile quite different from the living animal. The huge head disappears, and the skull becomes recognizably mammalian. The baleen whales have immense jawbones, curved like the tusks of elephants. In Norway, they are used as arched gateways by whalers who cherish souvenirs. Like most mammals, from mice to giraffes, whales have seven neck vertebrae. These are compressed and relatively rigid, although whales can nod and shake their heads. The body is made supple by extra vertebrae, cushioned by pads of cartilage, and though whales cannot quite bend to touch their tails, they are astonishingly flexible. Whales swim differently from fish, which move by swishing their tails from side to side. A whale beats its flukes up and down, like a frogman swimming with feet tied together. Some whales have a small dorsal fin and some no fin at all. They use their flippers not for swimming but to add balance and to help steer.

Whales solve the problem of breathing in a very special way. Moving the nostrils to the top of the head has required rearrangement of the bones of the skull. The nostrils, or blowholes, of baleen whales are two slits whose highly elastic sides normally seal out water. From the blowhole a nasal passage leads to the opening of the throat, just as in any mammal. Land mammals, however, cannot breathe and swallow at the same time. Whales can. The nasal passages of land beasts have specialized cells that filter out dust and moisten air, but since sea air is clean and moist, whales have dispensed with them. Whales have a larynx, or voice box, in the same place as other mammals but they have no vocal cords. One of the mysteries of cetology is how baleen whales make their diverse sounds. It is presumed to have something to do with exchanges of air between certain diverticula of air sacs that are part of the breathing apparatus.

When a whale surfaces and exhales, there is a visible spout, and the spout of each species has a characteristic size and shape, enabling whalers to tell the various species apart. The spout of the blue whale is a plume twenty feet high. Right whales, another baleen species, blow two spouts, which form a V. The spout is visible not because the whale has inhaled water but because when gas under pressure escapes it becomes cool and moist and turns to droplets; thus, vapor from the lungs of the whale condenses in the air like a man's breath on a cold day. The lungs of a blue whale weigh as much as a ton, but relative to the size of the whale's body they are rather small. The whale makes up for this, to some extent, by emptying and refilling its lungs almost completely with each breath. The small lung capacity is also compensated for by large oxygen storage capacity in the bloodstream and muscles and by an ability the whale possesses to divert circulation on occasion from the parts of the body that can endure lack of oxygen and to send the oxygen directly to the heart and brain, which must be continuously supplied.

Most of the food of baleen whales is concentrated in the upper layers of water and they do not normally dive very deep, but sometimes the whales may go down a thousand feet or more. A fin whale, the second-largest of the baleen species, has been struck by a harpoon with a pressure gauge attached and, in the subsequent dive, has carried harpoon and instrument to a recorded depth of a hundred and ninety-four fathoms (1,164 feet). A humpback has been found entangled in an underwater cable at sixty fathoms (360 feet). Baleen whales usually stay underwater for four to seven minutes between breaths, but, naturally, a whale's breathing rhythm changes with exertion. A whale that is being chased pants like a running horse and must surface more often, and thus fast catcher boats are able to force the creatures to the surface to be shot.

Any animal's body is seventy per cent water, and that water's salinity is far lower than seawater's. Fish get rid of extra salt through their gills. It is something of a mystery how whales manage, but the probability is that they excrete the salt with the help of very large kidneys. Whales do not drink water but absorb it from their food.

THE senses of baleen whales have not been studied, but much can be inferred from investigations of dolphins. In both sorts of whale, toothed and baleen, hearing is believed to be the sense on which they rely the most. Water is an excellent medium for sound, which travels four and a half times as fast there as in air. Whalers have long been aware that whales have acute hearing, but this faculty was not studied scientifically until the fifties, when dolphins were shown to have an acuteness of hearing second only to that of bats. Like bats, dolphins and other toothed whales have the ability to perceive objects by echolocation; that is, by bouncing vibrations off the objects and picking up the returning sound waves in the manner of sonar. Dolphins can perform astonishing feats through echolocation, such as finding a nickel on the bottom of a pool or discriminating between two sorts of metal. There is no evidence so far that baleen whales also echolocate; neither is there any evidence that they do not.

The cetacean ear is hardly visible. The external ear has disappeared, leaving simply a hole about the diameter of pencil lead; the aural canal is the size of a piece of string. In order for any creature to tell the direction of a sound, each ear must receive it independently, with the brain noting the fractional difference in arrival time and intensity. A man underwater can hear sound, but, because his skull bones conduct vibrations, it seems to come from everywhere at once. To obviate this, acoustic isolation of the ear is needed, and whales have achieved it with cavities, filled with albuminous foam, that isolate the middle ear from the surrounding bones. Dolphins, and probably all whales, have excellent directional hearing. A mystery of the whale's ear is that the semicircular canals, which provide a sense of balance, are remarkably small—no larger in a dolphin than in a hamster.

In the progressively greater darkness under the surface of the sea, eyes are far less useful than ears. Only ten per cent of the light striking the surface penetrates as far down as thirty feet; at that depth a big whale could not see its fluke before its face. Below two hundred and fifteen fathoms (twelve hundred and ninety feet) there is total darkness. The eyes of whales are adapted to enhance vision in dim light. They have a well-developed *tapetum lucidum*, or reflective backing to the eye, which makes the eye shine in the dark, and they have more, and longer, light receptors, or rods, than most mammals. Whales have no need for eyebrows, eyelashes, or tears to protect their eyes from dust and sweat, but they do have eyelids for protection; the outer layer of the cornea is made of tough cells and is bathed in an oily secretion. The vision of baleen whales has not been tested, but dolphins, for instance, can catch food flung to them and perform other tricks which show that, out of water at least, they see very well.

Fish can smell underwater, but if whales inhaled water they would drown. Consequently, their smelling apparatus has atrophied and all but disappeared. It is possible that baleen whales, which have vestiges of olfactory structures, can detect smells when their blowholes are out of water, but smell probably has little function in their lives.

There has been a great deal of speculation about the brain of the whale, which is strikingly large and convoluted. The brains of toothed whales are relatively larger than those of baleen whales. The largest brain on record is that of a sperm whale. It weighed 19.6 pounds. A hundred-ton blue whale had a brain weighing 15.25 pounds. Large animals have large brains, but intelligence as we think of it does not necessarily rise proportionately. Next to the whale, the elephant possesses the largest brain. It averages eleven pounds. A human brain weighs three pounds. Most biologists believe that the brains of whales are primarily devoted to acoustic perception rather than to deep thought. In the nineteen-sixties, a neurologist, Dr. John C. Lilly, created quite a popular stir with his theories about the marvellous mental faculties of dolphins and the possibility of meaningful communication between whales and men. Dolphins do indeed exhibit remarkable capacities, but Dr. Lilly's ideas are not taken seriously by most of the scientific community. Dr. Lilly himself has abandoned dolphins for mystical studies in California.

Whales are herd animals. The social life of dolphins seems to be intense and complicated. Far less is known about that of baleen whales, but it is clear that they communicate with and respond to each other, though they are spread out over wide stretches of water. Blue whales and several other species of baleen whales are thought to be monogamous. Females defend their calves fiercely. It is well established that toothed whales sometimes come to the aid of a wounded comrade, lifting it with their heads and supporting it in the water. Baleen whales, too, have been recorded as trying to help each other in moments of distress. These episodes are among the rare moments in which a whale reacts in a way that we can identify and sympathize with—though, unfortunately, it is usually done in response to human ferocity.

OF the ten species of baleen whales, six are grouped together in a family commonly known as the rorquals—from the Norwegian *rørhval*, or "tubed whale." *Hval*, like "whale," comes from the Anglo-Saxon word for "wheel," and describes the way whales seem to revolve as they surge through the water. The "tubes" are a series of deep pleats or grooves that mark their undersides from chin to navel. Most of the rorquals are long, graceful whales, streamlined from snout to flukes. Each of the species has a small, crescent dorsal fin and a powerful tail, which propels it at speeds that can exceed twenty miles an hour. The lower jaw is undershot, with the hard lower lip embracing the upper, which seems to fit into it as a lid fits into a teapot. A small brown eye is set near each corner of the mouth, where an upward groove suggests a smile. The species of rorquals descend in size from the gigantic blue whale to the middle-sized fin whale, and then to three smaller whales—the sei, Bryde's whale, and the minke. The humpback, which has a few pleats, is somewhere in the middle, although, being chunkier, it doesn't look like the other rorquals.

The rorquals range worldwide, though only Bryde's whale favors very warm waters, and the sei avoids the coldest regions. All are deep-water whales, feeding in the polar seas, north and south, and migrating to warmer water to give birth and mate. Their polar feeding grounds are well known because while they are feeding they congregate in certain areas, but when they disperse into the wide southern seas their trail is lost and they are seldom seen. The rorquals are too swift to be hunted from open boats, and in death their corpses sink. They were not hunted until modern technology provided fast boats and a method of inflating a dead whale with compressed air to keep it afloat. The modern age of whaling dawned in the eighteen-sixties with the perfection, by Svend Foyn, a Norwegian whaler, of the explosive harpoon fired by a gun. The Norwegians first used it to harvest the blue whales and fin whales in the North Atlantic. As these became scarce, the hunters shifted their attention to the gold mine of whales in the Antarctic. Starting in 1904, the destruction of rorquals began.

An ancient Phoenician word for "whale" meant "lord of the fish," and this surely applies to the largest rorqual, the blue whale. Longer than a railroad passenger car and twenty feet high at the midsection, it is by far the largest living creature, and perhaps the largest creature that has ever lived. (In size, the blue whale easily outclasses even the greatest of the dinosaurs, but it may have been equalled by an extinct shark whose fossilized teeth indicate a monumental size.) The largest blue whale on record was 110.8 feet long, and until twenty or thirty years ago such a size was more common than it is today. In the recent twilight of the species, though, few blue whales have lived long enough to grow anywhere near that big. Weighing a blue whale is a herculean task that can be accomplished only by cutting up the whale and weighing the pieces, and this has not been done often. The heaviest one weighed came to 134.25 tons. However, blue whales gain and lose gigantic amounts of weight according to the season. In their polar summer, they eat constantly and may gain thirty or forty tons, which is metabolized during a subsequent period of fasting. Blue whales generally cruise at six to eight miles per hour, but they can steam along at more than twice this speed for several hours. If they are frightened, they can surge forward at more than twenty miles an hour. A harpooned blue whale has pulled a ninety-foot boat, with its engines going full speed astern, for seven hours over fifty miles of ocean.

Blue whales are actually a mottled slate color, paler underneath. They sometimes turn yellow when a film of algae blooms on their skin; hence they have been called sulphur-bottom whales. They like deep water and seldom approach shore, but occasionally one is stranded. In 1922, a huge blue whale entered the Panama Canal, where it was machine-gunned by a military vessel. Blue whales are monogamous, often travel in pairs, and sometimes assemble in groups of five or six, but there are no large herds. When whalers find a pair of blue whales, they try to shoot the female first since the male will not desert her, but the female may be less staunch and leave the wounded male. Young blue whales are inquisitive, and when a catcher boat approaches them they often swim toward their executioners.

There may have been two hundred thousand blue whales in the Antarctic when whaling there began to achieve its peak, in the nineteen-twenties. The catch of blues rose annually, to a high point of 29,410 in the 1930–31 season, and declined thereafter, until in the 1964–65 season whalers found only twenty blue whales to kill. At that point, the International Whaling Commission decided that protection was in order. The present number of blue whales is unknown. They are occasionally sighted in all oceans, and optimists estimate that there are several thousand—enough to keep the species alive—but pessimists suggest that the remnant may dwindle to zero. No one can say whether the blue whale will ever return to its former abundance, or, if it does, how many hundreds of years that might take.

The humpback is a great, chunky beast, around fifty feet long, with a huge head and a small, rounded dorsal fin, which gives the whale a hump-backed appearance when it dives. The humpback usually has a black back and various piebald patches of white on its underside—a gaily parti-colored whale, with no two quite alike. A so-far inexplicable feature of the humpback is a series of knobs or bumps on its head and jaws and on the edge of its flippers. Each knob sprouts one or two coarse bristles, and it is possible that these function in some way as sense organs. The humpback has winglike flippers, which are sometimes as long as fifteen feet —far longer than those of any other whale. There are humpbacks in both the northern and the southern oceans, and they migrate from the poles to the equator, occasionally following the shorelines of the continents. In our part of the world, the humpback migrates from Newfoundland along the eastern seaboard to Bermuda and the Caribbean. In the Southern Hemisphere, the humpbacks move from the Antarctic to Australia, New Zealand, South America, and Africa. The humpback is a slow swimmer and can easily be caught by primitive methods; consequently, humpbacks have been hunted not only in their polar feeding grounds but from shore stations along their routes. With these whales attacked everywhere, their stocks all over the world have been reduced to a remnant. As recently as 1963, whalers killed 2,339 humpbacks in the North Pacific, and in the 1962–63 season, 270 in the Antarctic. Then, in 1963, when there were few left to kill, the whaling nations agreed to stop the slaughter in the Antarctic. The killing in the North Pacific was not stopped until 1966. By rough estimate, a species whose numbers may have originally been more than a hundred thousand has been reduced to five thousand or so.

The humpback is the most athletic and playful of the giants. It leaps and falls flat on its side or back, smacking the water with a gargantuan splash. Sometimes it swims on its back or turns a whole somersault above the water. A whaling captain, Charles Scammon, writing of experiences in the mid-nineteenth century, when humpbacks were plentiful, described their behavior thus: "In the mating season they are noted for their amorous antics. At such times their caresses are of the most amusing and novel character. . . . When lying by the side of each other, the *megapteras* [humpbacks] frequently administer alternate blows with their long fins, which love-pats may, on a still day, be heard at a distance of miles. They also rub each other with these same huge and flexible arms, rolling occasionally from side to side, and indulging in other gambols which can easier be imagined than described." It is perhaps not surprising that such a lively whale also emits the most musical sounds of any whale so far recorded. Scientists listening with hydrophones have discovered that humpbacks sing long, complicated songs that have some of the qualities of slightly mad orchestral music and some of the qualities of a gigantic bird singing in a gigantic birdbath.

M Y quest for a glimpse of great whales first took me to Bermuda, where Dr. Payne and his wife, Katy, were recording the sounds of humpbacks from a forty-four-foot motor sailer named the *Rockfish*, which had been lent them by Dr. Henry Clay Frick, a New York surgeon, who is a grandson of the steel millionaire, is a trustee of the New York Zoological Society, and has a home in Bermuda. On a choppy, windy April day, we set off from a harbor on the east end of the island, heading down along the south shore toward Challenger Bank, where the Paynes had had good luck finding humpback whales on previous trips. On board were the captain, a ruddy-faced Bermudian named Campbell O'Connor; the Paynes; Jane Frick, Dr. Frick's daughter, who is in her twenties, likes to take underwater photographs, and hopes to get some of whales; and Oliver Brazier, a quiet Bostonian who is an expert on electronic equipment. Roger Payne is a tall, dark-eyed, boyish-looking man in his late thirties, with the ability to alternate intense seriousness with easy and graceful humor. He has passionate personal feelings about whales, and writes and talks of them with a romantic eloquence that raises the hackles of some of his fellow-biologists. Most cetologists have started out as fishery men. Haddock and herring are not such stuff as dreams are made of, and these men have viewed whales primarily as a problem in population dynamics. They have wished to save whales only to make the maximum "use" of them. Payne, who has been crusading to save whales for the sake of whales, rather than having them used as a cheap food for mink—or even for men, since he considers it wicked to encourage the further overpopulation that menaces the globe—has a quite different point of view. His initial interest, after his graduation from Harvard, was in animal behavior, and he began by doing research on the hearing of bats, insects, and owls. He was diverted to whales by an emotional experience that occurred early in his career when he was on the staff of Tufts University. Late one sleety March night when he was working in his laboratory, he heard on the radio that a dead whale had washed ashore on Revere Beach. On an impulse, he drove out to see it. Later, he wrote about standing on the deserted beach at the water's edge, looking at the whale in the beam of a flashlight:

Payne

It was a small whale—a porpoise about eight feet long, with lovely, subtle curves glistening in the cold rain. It had been mutilated. Someone had hacked off its flukes for a souvenir and two other people had carved their initials deeply into its side. Someone else had stuck a cigar butt into its blowhole. I removed the cigar and I stood there for a long time with feelings I can't describe. Everybody has some such experience that affects him for life, probably several. That night was one of mine. At some point the flashlight went out, but as the tide came in I could periodically see the graceful outline of the whale against the white foam cast up by the waves. Although it is more typical than not of what happens to whales when they encounter man, that experience was somehow the last straw, and I decided to use the first possible opportunity to learn enough about whales so I might have some effect on their future.

When Payne found that humpback whales congregate off Bermuda in winter and early spring, he and his wife made a trip there in 1967. They met Frank Watlington, then an engineer with the Columbia University Geophysical Field Station at Bermuda. Some time before, hydrophones had been installed in the ocean offshore from Watlington's office, which is on a rocky headland, to record whatever sounds came along. He had been startled to find that these included medleys of a sort of unearthly singing, grunting, wailing, and rumbling, which he could attribute only to the humpbacks that were to be seen breaching and spouting offshore at the time the sounds were recorded.

When Roger Payne, who plays the cello and loves music, heard Watlington's recordings of whale sounds, he was deeply stirred. As he later described it: "Katy and I first heard humpback sounds over the roar of a generator and blower. Even so, what we experienced in that crowded, noisy compartment were the most fascinating and beautiful sounds of the wild world I had ever heard." Watlington gave the Paynes copies of the

unpredictably, they said, and moments of excitement are followed by long stretches of nothing but rough water. My notes on the trip follow, beginning in the morning as the six of us, in the cockpit of the *Rockfish*, braced ourselves against the surging roll of the waves en route to the banks where the whales are most often found.

•

ROGER explains that his immediate goal is to find out how loud the whale sounds are and how far they can carry—fundamental information that would help explain the function of the sounds. He speculates that the sounds could be a means of recognition between individuals or could proclaim territory, provide contact between migrant groups, or be involved in sex recognition and attraction. Or perhaps some components of the whale's sounds could be used in echolocation, like the sonar clicks of porpoises. Is the song the whale's altimeter, telling it where it is in relation to the surface in the course of a dive? Roger suggests still another theory: "A whale herd is like a convoy of boats, and the whales can't afford to collide. Their skins are very delicate. Maneuvering such a bulk must be like trying to drive a giant trailer truck in traffic. I figure whales have to be alert and communicate rapidly and precisely."

Katy asks, "Is there a sound for left and one for right?"

Roger grins and says, "I wish I knew." He would love to know how complex the communications are, he continues. Can whales convey as much information as a honeybee, which can tell other bees precisely where to find a certain supply of food? Are different components of the whale sounds used for different purposes? Is there, perhaps, one sound for close maneuvering and another that, like bird song, simply says, "I am a healthy male and I would like to meet you"?

A little later, Roger says, "Whales have the most acoustically complex life possible—more than fish, which rely on vision." He wants to know how whales get around in a nonvisual world. The more wide-ranging and unpredictable the life of a whale is, the more need it has to communicate over long distances. The food of whales drifts randomly over featureless ocean, and in order not to compete with each other they must stay far apart while feeding. Roger theorizes that sound frees individuals from the need for close contact, so they can spread out, and make the most of the food supply. But, as nomads wandering over vast distances, unable to leave a track or a scent for others to follow, they have the problem of getting back together. "If they can shout information on where they are," Roger says, "then the whole sea becomes an enormous room."

Roger explains that there is something called "the deep sound channel"—a layer of water that confines sound so that it can carry as far as halfway around the world. The sound of a dynamite blast near Australia, for instance, was once picked up by a listening device off Bermuda several hours later. Roger speculates that whales may send their signals over hundreds of miles through the deep sound channel. He is distressed because the multitude of ships churning through the ocean nowadays—there are fourteen hundred in the North Atlantic on any given day—are polluting the seas with noise. The whir of their propellers is on the same sound wavelength as the whales' noises and may mess up whale communications.

I ask Roger what other aspects of whales' lives he wants to investigate. He says he wants to know everything—where they go, what they do at each stage of their lives, and why. "A biologist wants to become part of an animal's life. I would like to be a flea on the shoulder of a bat. That's impossible, but maybe somebody will invent a little capsule in which you could attach yourself to a whale. What I want is to be *with* whales as much as possible." He says that close observations are very difficult around Bermuda, where the water is rough and the whales are rather widely dispersed, but that he has found a place off the South American coast where southern right whales gather in calm water behind a barrier reef and can be watched at close quarters. He thinks that, with enough patience, a human being will be able to get as close to whales as George Schaller and Jane van Lawick-Goodall have got to apes. He thinks that if you hang around whales long enough the older ones will come to ignore you, and you can take advantage of the curiosity of the young. But if you chase, injure, or frighten an animal, he says, you're finished. A colleague told him that a lion that was forcibly tagged

1798483

didn't forget the incident for two years. On a previous expedition, Roger attempted to plant a pinger —a device that sends out a signal—in a humpback whale so that he could follow the whale, but it used its long flippers to wipe off the device. The episode frightened the whale and disturbed Roger. He has resolved to pursue his studies by methods that don't risk hurting his subjects.

Katy says that one of her objectives in analyzing whale songs is to find out whether individuals can be recognized by their songs—or, if not individuals, then groups. If so, they could be tracked by their songs, and their travels charted. She compares whale song to bird song, pointing out that because birds are so small their lives are speeded up. A bird song lasts only a few seconds—or, at most, a few minutes—and the notes are very close together. She thinks whales sing huge, slow songs appropriate to their size, and that is why each note is so distinct. It sounds to human ears like a record slowed down.

We are chugging along into rising swells, and the horizon is turbulent with whitecaps. Campbell O'Connor, our captain, says it is going to get rougher and now might be a good time to eat. Katy goes below and gets us crackers, cheese, and soup. While we eat, Roger explains how he hopes to gather information on the loudness of whale sounds. He wants to record a whale's voice on tape and then, when the whale surfaces, measure its distance from the boat. There are three things to be measured at the same time: the intensity of the sound as it reaches the hydrophones, the distance to the whale, and the temperature of the water, which influences sound conductivity. Measuring the distance to a singing whale is not easy. First, the whale must be identified as the one that is being heard through the earphones, and then its position must be fixed at a moment coinciding with a certain segment of the tape recording of its song. Roger has thought of various ways to measure the distance to the whale, but fears that some of them would frighten the whale into silence and flight. He has decided to try taking simultaneous pictures from two cameras fixed a certain distance apart, and calculating the angle between the two images. As he snaps the shutter, he will record an identifying number on the tape. The camera rig is lying on top of the deckhouse.

Katy shouts, "Whale!" Roger asks O'Connor to turn off the engine. The boat drifts and rolls in the choppy waves, which whisper and splash against its sides. Only the jib steadies us. Off to one side, there is a round slick, as if a ship had sunk. This is characteristic of a spot where a whale has gone down. Oliver Brazier, the sound expert, puts the hydrophones over the side. Roger, in bathing trunks and earphones, stands tensely in the heaving cockpit, listening, but reports that he is hearing only strumming interference.

"What direction was he going?" he asks.

"East," says O'Connor, pointing ahead. We are about two miles offshore.

Roger says, "I hear a very distant whale."

I picture a vast, green chamber beneath us, and

wonder if any person will ever be able to move in it as freely as the whales do. Roger and Oliver are fiddling with the equipment. When they finally decide that the machinery is working right, there is no whale.

O'Connor says, "That whale's got no time to mess with you people. He's gone to sing to his girl friend."

We raise the mainsail and go to look for other whales. We plow through the waves with white foam at our bow. We are all getting impatient, but see nothing except gray waves hurrying past us. Then O'Connor says, "There's one!" and points off the port bow. A second later, I see a whale spout. The spout is like a puff of smoke. It hangs in the air, then disintegrates. It comes again. We lower the mainsail, and Katy throws the hydrophones over. The whale stays under for what seems a long time —actually, it's only a few minutes—and then suddenly rises a stone's throw away. I see a gleaming black back and patches of brilliant white. Then it is gone, in a surge of foam. Roger is on top of the boom struggling with the cameras. Katy says, "I'm getting great sound, but it can't be this whale. It's too far away." She hands me the earphones. They are filled with sound. Mixed with the gurgle and wash of water I hear something like a baby crying very far away. Then the cry turns into a medley of ethereal calls such as tiny translucent fairies might make. Katy thinks we are hearing two or three whales at once. There is an impression, impossible to confirm, of calls and answers. The whale we saw doesn't appear again. What we are hearing *must* be far away. We settle down to wait for another strolling singer. In spite of the jib, we roll and slat as the gray seas come past like rolling mountains. Not far beneath us, there are real mountains, rising from a tremendous depth. They have flattened, mesalike tops that form banks a hundred and eighty feet below the surface. At the moment, I learn, we are over the saddle between Challenger and Plantagenet Banks. The valley floor is three or four thousand feet below the mountaintops, and the slopes are so steep, O'Connor says, that he once dropped bow and stern anchors in this area and found his bow in a hundred and eighty feet of water and his stern in five hundred. I wonder if the whales slide down the sides of the mountains, coasting like kids on snow, and then laze along the valley floor.

I ask how close we might get to a whale. Katy says that one year three whales headed straight for the boat. She jumped in the water with a mask on and, looking down, could see their giant forms and white-banded flippers gleaming right below her. She says she felt awfully small. And once, at the South American whale grounds, she and Brazier were in a small outboard motorboat when a whale came up, raised its head out of the water to peer at them, turned tail and flurried the water in threat, then thrust its flukes under the boat, lifted it into the air, and put it down. As they hit the surface, Oliver started the motor, and they scooted away. Katy noticed that there were two mother whales

Gray Whale 35 – 45 feet long

41

True Beaked Whale

Bottlenose Whale   35 feet long

42

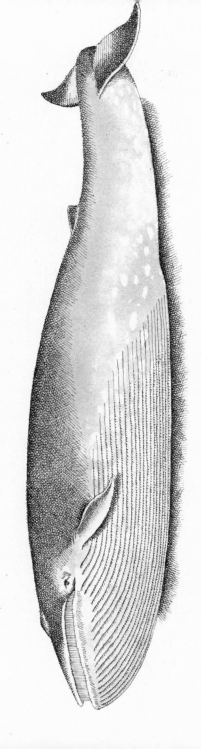

Blue Whale   80 – 100 feet long

43

Finback Whale   60 – 75 feet long

44

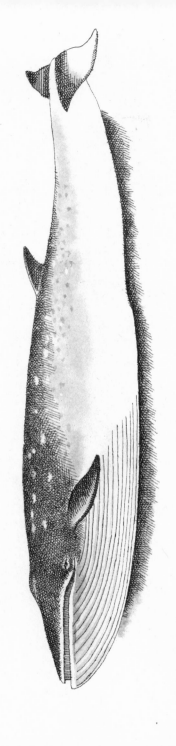

Sei Whale   50 – 60 feet long

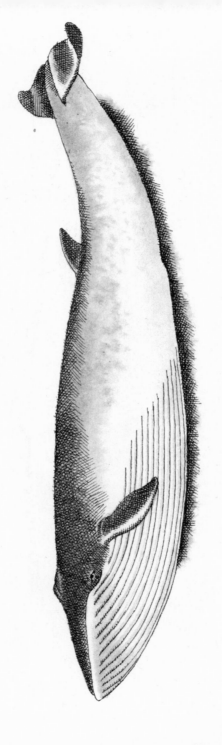

Bryde's Whale   35 – 40 feet long

46

Little Piked Whale   25 – 30 feet long

47

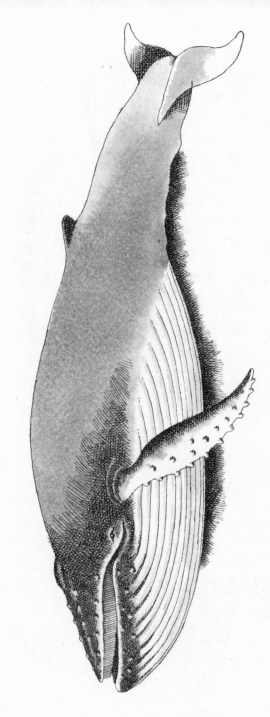

Humpback Whale   40 feet long

48

Sperm Whale 65 – 75 feet long

49

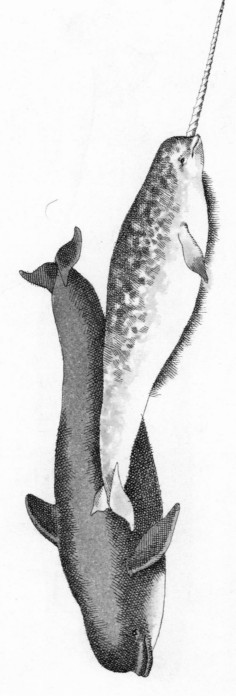

Narwhal   18 – 25 feet long

Pilot Whale   20 – 25 feet long

Killer Whale 28 – 32 feet long

Common Dolphin 22 feet long

Black Right Whale   50 – 60 feet long

52

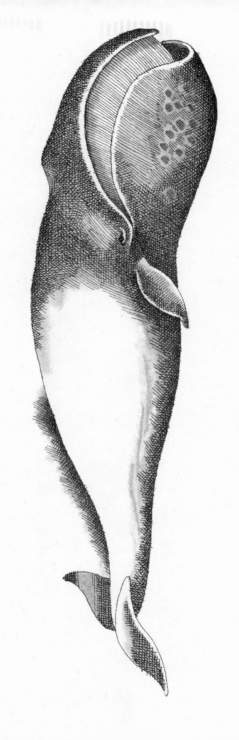

Greenland Right Whale   60 – 65 feet long

with calves nearby, and wondered if the whale that threatened them was a bull protecting females. It escorted them from the area. Roger says he had a similar experience when a whale followed his skiff and nudged the stern with its head. "My first reaction was delight," he recalls, "mixed with some alarm, but I decided to hang on and see what was going to happen next. Nothing did! The whale had found out what he wanted to know about me, and, I suspect, was also hanging on to see what was going to happen next. It was a marvellous meeting."

After an hour, no whale has appeared. We pull in the hydrophones and move on. Half an hour later, we haul the mainsail down again and put the hydrophones over. Katy listens, and immediately her face brightens. She says the whale sounds are very loud. Roger begins recording. I listen for a moment. There is a sound like the hinge on a creaky iron door. Then we hear what sounds like a high-low operatic duet. Is it really a duet or one whale talking to itself? Roger would give a lot to know. All at once, O'Connor sees a whale swimming parallel to us. It is surprisingly hard to estimate the distance of a whale from a boat, but this one looks huge and seems close—perhaps less than a hundred yards away. It blows. The great, gleaming black back surges out with a swift roll. There is a glimpse of the little fin near the tail, and then the whale is gone. The few minutes the whale is visible are intensely exciting and tantalizing. To be so close to something so enormous and so transient! There is a longing to detain it, explore it, touch it, make some contact—to say or do something that the whale will respond to.

Now there are four whales off the bow, blowing as they move away from us, while closer at hand two black torpedoes cut the water in front of us. The black backs roll out and under. Then three more whales appear, even closer, and they blow twice and make a leisurely turn around our stern. They are visible for a count of twelve. I can see the small eye and the smile at the corner of the mouth. Over the white bands on the flippers the water takes on a turquoise hue, as it does over white sand in the tropics. While these three are circling us, Roger thinks, they are within a hundred feet. We are up to our ears in whales—so many that there is no way to tell which are singing. Katy reports a great medley of sounds. I listen briefly, and hear groans, bleats, moos, even motorcycles starting up and receding into the distance. Now all the whales are gone. We feel left alone, like watchers when a parade has turned the corner, but through the earphones the whales can still be heard singing in the distance.

IT is afternoon now, and we have been hearing continuous song for an hour without seeing a whale. This indicates to Roger that either the sound comes from very far off or the whales are staying down a very long time. Katy lends me her earphones. I hear a slightly daft siren song. The sweetest, most poetic notes, pure and piercing, are followed by low ratchet sounds and Bronx cheers.

Next, there are haunted-house sounds—Cathy calling Heathcliff. Then a switch to a rural scene—somebody blowing into a jug, beagles yipping, cattle lowing.

I contemplate the endless motion of whales. They go through the water like perpetually turning wheels, doomed never to rest or to form any attachment to a single place. They are Flying Dutchmen. I mention this to Roger. He says that at the South American site the whales loll along the shore, circling there and resting on the current. Sometimes they lie on their backs and wave their gigantic flippers. He says it is a marvellous place to observe whale behavior, because you can stand on a cliff and look right down on the whales. He often saw contact between them—heads touching, sliding over each other. In greeting each other, the whales arch their backs in a peculiar way. He saw a mating. The female, with a calf beside her, lay in the water. The male slid smoothly beneath her, turned belly up, and arched his back. It lasted only a second. There are old reports of whales' mating in a vertical position, rising out of the water belly to belly, but Roger thinks that this is unlikely.

Roger's South American whales are right whales, and at this time in their lives they are silent. Humpbacks apparently cease to sing when they move to their northern feeding grounds, where they stay from May to December; sounds have been recorded, but they have not been found to be "songs." This summer silence is puzzling to Roger, but he notes that the whales are particularly scattered then, and it is harder to pick up their sounds. He wonders if perhaps they have been silenced by fear of large, noisy vessels from which recording has been attempted. He thinks it very important to approach whales in a sailboat.

Since whales have a larynx but no vocal cords, we discuss the mystery of how they make their sounds. People emit air to cause sound vibration, but there are other possible techniques—stridulation, for instance. The whale might strum a taut membrane inside itself. Roger, however, thinks it most likely that whales use air, because an air-filled cavity produces a harmonic series similar to whale sounds; namely, even multiples of the fundamental. This theory assumes that the whale transfers air inside it from one cavity to another, and implies the use of some sort of plumbing, probably in the head, for the purpose. Whales have a number of cavities associated with the larynx and the nasal passage which might serve to produce sound—and the sound need not necessarily come *out* of any particular aperture. It could simply emerge through the blubber and skin.

We've just seen a black back wheel out of the water. It is coming toward us, with a smaller one just behind—a mother and a calf. They are so close that as they submerge we again see the water turn turquoise over the gleaming white on their flippers. Their skin shines like divers' wet-suits. There is a wake of champagnelike bubbles, and smooth eddies behind it. The whales blow a deep, long, sighing exhalation, quite loud—first the mother and then the baby—and sink. They surface three more times, moving slowly away. Roger photographs them, but Katy hears nothing on the earphones.

We raise the sail and start for Challenger Bank. When we reach it, we haul down the sail and drop the hydrophones over. Bermuda is barely visible. There is a whale half a mile ahead. Katy hears a distant whale sound over the earphones. On the horizon behind us I suddenly see a cigar-shaped cylinder thrust out of the water to an incredible height, like the lift-off of a rocket. It is a whale standing on its tail. I yell, and everybody sees the giant splash as it topples and hits the water. Katy says the singing she was hearing in the earphones stopped about that time, and Roger thinks perhaps we have seen Katy's singing whale. He has a theory that whales sing when they are near the surface, rising and falling in shallow dives and not travelling fast. He thinks that they lie in the water and sing, and that the sound resembling a ratchet occurs when the whale is coming to the surface for a breath.

After a while, we start moving again. O'Connor says there are fishpots ahead, and predicts that we'll find whales among them. He says the whales like to rub their backs on the fishpots, which sometimes damages the pots' little marker flags and angers the fishermen, who often shoot at the whales. We approach a fishpot marked by a staff flying a pennant, which seems a strange touch of civilization in this empty wilderness of water. Suddenly we are in the midst of whales. A pair, with a third whale behind them, surge alongside and blow—one, two, three great sighing, steamy sounds, like those made by a steam locomotive settling down on a siding. I see an open blowhole quivering and vibrating. It is a couple of inches across. Jane has jumped overboard in her bluejeans and is paddling around like a seal, upright in the choppy water, wet hair streaming over her eyes, as she tries to adjust her camera. There is excited activity on board, with Katy and Oliver working the sound equipment and Roger taking pictures. The whales surge by. They surface and sink, surface and sink, with a rhythmic, easy roll that has a wonderful grace.

These whales go by very fast. I am reminded of being at the rail of a race track when the horses come swiftly toward you. For an extraordinary instant, they are right beside you, so that you smell the sweat and hear the panting and the creak of leather. Then they are going away. For just such an instant, the whales surface beside the boat and they hurry on past the bow, and abruptly decide to sound. They rise, then dive steeply, seeming to stand on their heads. Their huge flukes wave above the surface like the wings of giant black butterflies; then they sink smoothly into the sea and are gone. The waving flukes are a sign that they are heading for the depths. Everybody seems to feel very frustrated. Jane climbs back in the boat, having failed to get a picture. The deck is a tangle of wires, but the sounds that Katy heard over the earphones were distant ones and could not have been from these whales. Roger has good pictures but no whale sounds to match them.

After a dismal, letdown hour of sloshing around, we motor to a spot near another bunch of fish traps. Roger puts on earphones. He reports that he has briefly heard a whale singing, but it has quit. "I'm afraid we shut it up with the motor," he says. After a minute, his face brightens. "Watch for a blow," he says. "There's somebody close." We watch in vain. Though the sounds are tantalizingly clear, an hour or so passes and we see nothing. Now it seems miraculous that we saw the other whales so close.

We move again, and as soon as the hydrophones are down Katy reports that she hears some beautiful grunts. She passes me the earphones, and I hear sounds exactly like water chugging out of a bottle. Then comes the siren song. Now I picture dark-green corridors lined with mirrors, and sirens in diaphanous white garments drifting through them. Jane yells "Breach!" and I turn my head in time to see a giant splash a few hundred yards astern. The whale rises again, and almost its entire body is visible. It hangs above the water for an instant and falls with a loud report, amid geysers of water. It vanishes. We wait hopefully, but it doesn't reappear. Apparently, it is also silent. The sounds on the hydrophones are coming from a distance. I hand the earphones back to Katy, who sits watching the water and listening. At intervals, she says, "It's so beautiful!"

•

MY notes on the trip end there, but I remember, perhaps best of all, what came afterward.

For several hours, we drifted over the banks, rolling steadily but less furiously than in the early afternoon. An evening calm was settling on the water. Now and then, we saw a distant spout—nothing close. (Roger suspects that a whale can exhale invisibly underwater and then surface just long enough to take a breath without being seen.) Katy sat in the stern, resting against a pile of life jackets, listening. The sun sank, and the sky and water turned mauve and gray. O'Connor planned to let us drift through the night. He lit the running lights and went below to get some supper. Oliver and Roger went down to work with the recording equipment. They wanted to run the recorder all night.

I sat in the cockpit, watching the light soften and turn silver, watching the ceaseless movement of the water, and becoming aware that our boat was shrinking—that it had become a very small platform to rest on in this endless ocean. As I gazed at the metallic surface of the waves, it occurred to me that in the fifty million years that whales have existed the land has changed beyond recognition but the sea has remained a primeval landscape, and may have looked just like this at the beginning of creation. The sky was empty. There were no clouds to keep us company, and no birds.

Katy put down the earphones and went below. After a moment, I moved to her place and put them on. Whale songs were coming through beautifully. They were lovely and fascinating, but what struck me most of all was that they had the warmth of life. The cold, empty world of the surface dropped away as I dipped into the populated depths. Far from being empty, the great chamber below was filled with life. I relaxed as I listened to its lively hum. It was like looking through a pane of glass, watching busy activities on the other side, yet not being quite able to enter. I thought about the various speculations as to why whales make their strange sounds, and the answer suddenly seemed clear: they sing their songs so that they won't be alone.

THE key element in the existence of the great whales is, of course, their food supply. In certain regions of the ocean, plankton, made up of a variety of small, drifting plants and of tiny animals, the most common of which is krill, grows with fantastic speed and abundance. The other very large sea creatures—the forty-foot basking shark, the fifty-foot whale shark, and the huge manta ray—also depend on plankton. Since plankton is so abundant—two hundred million tons of krill alone are produced annually, or nearly three times the tonnage of sea creatures that human beings harvest—it has been suggested that we might harvest plankton and eat it ourselves, but so far no one has produced an acceptable food made of krill. Whales, of course, harvest krill with consummate efficiency, and it has been pointed out that for us to destroy whales and eat krill is the equivalent of destroying cattle so that we can eat their grass. All life in the sea, as on land, depends on plants, which alone can synthesize organic matter from carbonic acid, sunlight, and water. But whereas the tropical land areas produce the most luxuriant plant life, things are reversed in the sea, and cold waters are the richest. This is because cold water holds more dissolved oxygen and carbonic acid than warm water does, and also because the surface water near the poles contains an especially rich supply of plant nutrients, derived from the bodies of dead organisms and other waste products. Normally, this debris sinks to the bottom, but in the polar regions there are vast areas of upwelling water—currents from the deep rising abruptly to the surface—which endlessly bring up supplies of food for the tiny plants floating in the sunlit surface layer. Thus, the cold, gray polar seas are in fact bubbling springs of life, thousands of times as productive as the transparent blue waters of the tropical oceans. The sea plants, thriving in the almost endless sunshine of the polar summer, provide pasture for a host of small grazing organisms: worms, snails, jellyfish, and shrimp. One of the most abundant, particularly in the Antarctic, is the shrimplike crustacean *Euphausia superba* Dana—otherwise, krill. In the high latitudes, krill can occur in fantastic concentrations, forming a rusty-red carpet thirty feet thick over several square miles of ocean. Krill is the staple food of baleen whales, and the amounts of it they consume are fantastic. It is not unusual for the stomach of a blue whale to contain a ton of krill.

The seasonal cycle of the rorqual is tied to the summer harvest of krill and other plankton in polar waters. For three months or so, the whales graze through the long polar days, storing up riches in the form of fat. Females with young wean them in the midst of this abundance. Pregnant females are able to nourish the unborn young at a rate that permits tremendous growth within the womb. As autumn darkness falls and the pastures of plankton wither, the whales move toward the equator in a migration of thousands of miles. Though they eat little or nothing, they are still fat and strong as they approach the equator—in prime condition for the great physiological demands of mating and nursing that lie ahead. When they reach warm water, the females that have weaned calves during the summer mate again and begin gestation. Pregnant females give birth in the warm water.

No one has yet seen the birth of a baleen whale, but it is generally believed that the calf is born tail first, so that there is no risk of its taking a lungful of water during birth. Dolphin mothers quickly push the newborn to the surface, and probably baleen whales do, too. The nipples of the female whale are recessed in openings on either side of the genital slit, and are equipped with muscles that squirt milk into the mouth of the calf. The calf, which lacks soft lips, seizes the teat between tongue and palate. Whale milk is creamy white, slightly fishy in taste, and very rich—three or four times as concentrated as cow's milk. It has been guessed that a big whale gives more than a hundred and thirty gallons a day. Infant whales are huge babies by any standard. A newborn blue whale weighs two tons and is twenty-five feet long—almost a third of the length of its mother. Every day while it is nursing, it grows two inches and gains two hundred pounds. It can swim capably from birth, and during the nursing period sticks close to its mother's side.

The age at which the great whales reach sexual maturity is not definitely known; it is thought that blue whales and fin whales reach puberty when they are six years old, at which time they have completed eighty-five per cent of their growth. The rate at which females produce young is likewise uncertain. Species probably differ; some may give birth every year, some every two years, and some every three years. Examination of dead females has revealed scars on the ovaries which are thought to correspond to the number of times the whales have ovulated, but the scars do not indicate over what period of time the ovulations have taken place. The only clue to the age of a mature baleen whale is found in a waxy earplug that appears to add layers throughout the whale's lifetime. But how often a layer is added—whether every six, twelve, or eighteen months, or every two years—has not been established. Also unknown is the natural life span of whales. In most mammals, childhood occupies an eighth to a sixth of the total life expectancy. This would indicate an age of thirty-five or forty years for whales. An old harpoon found in a right whale has been identified after forty years and one in a sperm whale has been identified after thirty-two years, but, naturally, these findings do not indicate how much longer the whales might have lived.

The birthrate of whales is of paramount interest to cetologists, because therein lies the key to the numbers of individuals that whalers can kill without exterminating the species. In all animal populations, more individuals are born than the environment can sustain. Thus, a certain percentage of each species is a surplus that can be killed (or "harvested," as those in the trade prefer to call it) without affecting the crop of young the following year. This possible crop, year after year, is called the sustainable yield. If it is exceeded, the remaining breeding stock cannot make up the loss, and the population shrinks. This smaller population has an even smaller sustainable yield, and so on. If the latter number continues to be exceeded, the population inevitably sinks to zero. To find the magic number—sustainable yield—it is necessary to know the number of animals at a given time in the basic stock, the death rate, and the birthrate. In dealing with whales, scientists are sure of only one of these factors—the death rate. It can be safely assumed that very few great whales of the hunted species escape the hunters to die of old age; therefore, the number recorded as killed by the whalers is near the actual death rate. Neither of the other figures essential for an accurate estimate of sustainable yield has been established. The total population of each species is roughly estimated from the number of sightings. The birthrate is guessed at from examination of the ovaries of females, but the interpretation of these data is open to dispute. It can thus be fairly said that the men who annually set the quota of whales that can be killed "safely," without jeopardizing the stock, actually have very little idea of what they are doing. For almost twenty years, disinterested scientists have warned that the rate of killing was quite likely more than the stocks could sustain, and year after year their predictions of shrinking stocks of whales have been confirmed. The industry has ignored the warnings, on the ground that "proof" of overkilling was still lacking. In the case of the Japanese, the industry maintains captive scientists who regularly provide optimistic interpretations of the data to bolster the view that there are still plenty of whales left to kill.

THE rarest of all the great whales—so rare that it is seldom seen, and is seldom even mentioned except in scientific papers now and then—is the right whale. The North Atlantic right whale and its close relative the Greenland right whale were the first to be hunted to near extinction. The right whale is a massive, slow whale, easy to catch from an open boat, and hence it was the earliest to be attacked by primitive hunters everywhere. When it is dead, its carcass floats, and for this reason, as well as its slowness and high oil content, it became known as the "right" whale to catch. The right whale is short and stocky—a sixty-foot specimen may be forty feet around the waist—with a huge head, which makes up almost a third of the body length. The mouth is acutely curved and is cavernous. The baleen, perhaps twenty feet long and sixteen wide, hangs from the upper jaw like fringe. Some right whales produce a thunderous bellow, like a bull, that is easily heard without earphones by any close bystander. The right whale also has mysterious bumps on its chin and snout, and a large horny growth on top of its head, which is known as the bonnet.

Right whales once swam by the thousand in the temperate waters of both the Atlantic and the Pacific. The Japanese hunted them from shore from the earliest times. In Europe, major commercial whaling began in the eleventh century in the Bay of Biscay, which then teemed with right whales. The Basques were the first whalers, but other Europeans soon joined in, and by the sixteenth century they had destroyed the stock on their coasts of the Atlantic. A couple of hundred years later, American whalers did the same on our coasts. On the other side of the world, the rights were given a little more time, but in the nineteenth century a great fleet of whaling ships of many nations swept the Pacific, both north and south, and polished off the right whales there within fifty years. The fact that the right whale is so rare and yet still exists poses an interesting question for biologists. Why is it that although it has not been hunted in a hundred years it has multiplied so little? Or, on the other hand, why has it not gone under entirely? If the other baleen whales follow its example, the stocks may never regenerate.

As the black right whale became scarce in European waters, the Greenland right whale was discovered. In 1596, a Dutch ship exploring the Arctic in search of the Northwest Passage to the Orient brought back the news that the waters around the Arctic islands of Novaya Zemlya, Spitsbergen, and Jan Mayen were teeming with whales. The Greenland whale closely resembles the black right whale except that its head is even more huge and its mouth more grotesquely curved. In 1820, a whaling captain named William Scoresby, Jr., published an account of his experiences in the North Atlantic, and described the Greenland whale, or bowhead, thus: "When the mouth is open, it presents a cavity as large as a room, and capable of containing a merchant-ship's jollyboat, full of men, being six or eight feet wide, ten or twelve feet high (in front), and fifteen or sixteen feet long. . . ." Its habitat is in the Arctic seas, where it swims amid the floating ice, easily pushing great floes apart. Greenland whales often swim under the ice, breaking through with their backs in order to breathe. Sometimes they are trapped and perish, to the delight of Eskimos who happen to find them. Greenland whales do not migrate far beyond the Arctic regions but give birth in icy waters. Their calves are protected by an extraordinarily thick layer of blubber.

British and Dutch fleets began to hunt Greenland whales in the early sixteen-hundreds. The profits were huge. A single whale yielded twenty-five tons of oil and a ton and a half of whalebone—enough to pay for the trip. Other Europeans joined in the hunt, and the industry boomed. Hundreds of ships and thousands of men participated. As the nearer stocks were eliminated, the fleets moved westward. In the eighteenth century, the Americans began Arctic whaling, moving into the North Pacific in the nineteenth century, killing black right whales, and completing the encirclement of the Greenland whales. By the end of the nineteenth century, the Greenland whales were almost gone, and most countries gave up the hunt. The British, however, persevered, devising better equipment, pursuing the very last whales into the deepest ice, and slaughtering all sizes indiscriminately. They did not desist until 1912, when an expedition found not a single whale. However, a handful had escaped into the vastness of the Arctic waters, and they are slowly coming back in the western Arctic region, and now and then a Greenland whale is seen in Hudson Bay and, more frequently, the Bering Sea. Eskimos or Siberian natives capture ten or twenty a year, and they are spotted from ships. Between the first whaling in the Bay of Biscay and the virtual destruction of the black and Greenland right whales all over the world, eight hundred years had passed—a long time by modern standards. We are now accomplishing the same sort of slaughter in a fraction of that time.

The fin whale lacks the glamour of the blue, since it is only the second-largest of the whales, but, at seventy-five or eighty-five feet, and weighing fifty-five tons, it is nevertheless a tremendous creature and a fine quarry for whalers. It is the slimmest, most elegant rorqual, with a pointed snout and tail and a sickle-shaped dorsal fin. Its back is a dark, slaty gray that may look black as it surges out of water—or greenish, owing to a film of algae—and its body shades to creamy white on the underside. The pleats make gray furrows from chin to midsection. An odd feature of the fin whale's color pattern is that the right side of the lower jaw is always very light and the left side very dark. Like the blue whale, the fin ranges all oceans, but it does not move quite as far into the polar ice in summer or as close to the equator in winter. Its wintering grounds are evidently in the deep oceans, and its wanderings, like those of the blue, have not been accurately charted. In the North Atlantic, it has been found all along the coasts of the continents. It is more inclined to eat fish than is the blue—which generally subsists on krill alone—and follows fish closer to shore. It often feeds while swimming on its side with its mouth open, then turns on its back with its lower jaw partly out of water as it swallows.

Fin whales can swim as fast as blues or faster. A harpooned fin whale was once clocked speeding off at thirty-one miles per hour, and a fin whale whose dorsal fin had been shot off in an initial encounter was killed five days later more than five hundred miles away. Fin whales do not breach unless they are wounded or excited, but then their entire length may shoot out of the water. They are usually not very gregarious, swimming alone or in groups of three or four, but now and then, in the days when they were plentiful, they would gather by the dozen, the score, or even the hundred, to the satisfaction of the whalers. Then their spouts, like white plumes, would flash everywhere against the gray sky of the Antarctic seas.

Originally, fin whales were the most plentiful of the rorquals. There were once perhaps a quarter million in the southern oceans. As the blue whales became scarcer, the whalers turned to fins, killing them at the rate of twenty or thirty thousand a year. Now the annual catch is below three thousand a year, and some scientists think that the fin, like the blue, is an endangered species; recently, the International Whaling Commission at last called for a halt to the killing. Until then, at least, those in the Atlantic were still killed from shore stations.

Now, with the blue whale almost gone and the fin whale greatly reduced, the whalers are turning to the small rorquals for their harvest. The sei and Bryde's whale are much alike. Both are about fifty feet long and look like small fin whales; Bryde's whale, which is rarer, is found mainly off the coast of South Africa. The sei, so named by the Norwegians because it appeared along the coast at the same time as a kind of fish called the *seje*, ranges from pole to pole but avoids the coldest water. Its migrations seem to be less regular than those of the larger whales, and now and then seis appear in an unaccustomed spot. Long ago, when they were plentiful, there were sudden, inexplicable congregations of sei whales, as though a convention had been called. In the spring of 1885, thousands appeared off Finnmark, in northern Norway, and stayed the summer, even though the natives killed them by the hundred. They came again in 1898, but no such astonishing aggregation has been recorded recently.

The sei is equipped with baleen that ends in fringe as soft and fine as fleece, with which it can strain very small creatures out of the water. In the Pacific, however, it often eats small fish. It twists and turns its lithe body as it pursues its prey. For short sprints, the sei is the fastest whale, and when it is harpooned it thrashes mightily, which has given it a bad name among whalers.

Because seis yield less oil than bigger whales, they were not heavily hunted in earlier days. The world catch from 1909 to 1949 was 35,908—only a small fraction of the number of blues and fins killed in that time. Most of the seis were killed off the coasts of Japan and Korea. The Chinese think the sei is the best eating of all whales. Intensive killing of seis began in the early nineteen-sixties, and perhaps half the original stock in the Antarctic, estimated at a hundred and fifty thousand, has been killed. Seis have also been hunted heavily in the North Pacific. The International Whaling Commission has finally set a quota for the killing—seventy-five hundred for 1973–74—but many experts believe that this runs true to I.W.C. form and is too high.

The smallest rorqual is called the little piked whale, or minke, the latter name immortalizing, derisively, a Norwegian gunner who shot one he mistook for a blue—a mistake his shipmates found amusing, since the little piked whale is only thirty feet long. It looks like a diminutive fin whale but it has a distinguishing white band across the flippers. It ranges high latitudes around the world and goes deeper into the Antarctic than any other whale. In 1908, Sir Ernest Henry Shackleton, a British explorer, named the Bay of Whales after discovering vast numbers of minkes gambolling among the ice floes there. Assemblages of a thousand have been seen. The minke is a frolicsome whale, and jumps right out of water, or stands vertically to look about. Sometimes it will rest its head on a floe. Minkes break the ice to make breathing holes, but quite often, in spite of the whales' efforts to keep these open, they freeze over and the whales are drowned.

In the Northern Hemisphere, the minke visits the coast of Europe, and some have even swum up the Thames to London. It is the whale most frequently stranded on the British coast. When bigger whales were plentiful, minkes were not heavily hunted except off Norway and Japan. Between 1938 and 1954, the Norwegians killed 37,716. It is believed that there is still a sizable population—three hundred thousand—in the Antarctic, where a quota of five thousand has now been set by the

I.W.C. Thus, these small whales provide economic insurance for continued voyages in the course of which the remnants of the bigger species are taken.

Of all the baleen whales, the one that is most easily seen and studied is the gray whale, which parades along the California coast on its migrations between its summer pasture in the Bering Sea and its winter quarters on the coast of Baja California. En route, the gray can be watched from shore or counted from airplanes, and a fairly accurate tally of its numbers is possible. The gray whale constitutes a family in itself. It has more hair (one gray whale had sixty hairs on its head and a hundred and twenty on its lower jaw) and a slightly more flexible body. Over all, the gray is a slim whale, forty or so feet long and rather cigar-shaped, with a small head. The mouth neatly divides the head into two equal parts. Gray whales have from two to four pleats on the throat, and so are intermediate between right whales, which lack pleats, and the rorquals, which have from forty to a hundred. Gray whales occur only in the Pacific, and there are, or were, two stocks—those seen on the California coast and a separate group that migrated between Korea and the Sea of Okhotsk—which the Japanese have to all intents and purposes destroyed.

The California gray whales, too, were nearly exterminated, but they have made a remarkable recovery. It has been estimated that between twenty-five thousand and fifty thousand gray whales originally frequented the California coast. As settlers reached the area, they opened shore stations and fell upon the whales. Beginning in the eighteen-fifties, thousands were killed each year, including nursing mothers and young. With the discovery of their breeding grounds, in Baja California, the slaughter intensified. Within forty years, the gray whales had very nearly disappeared, and the industry collapsed. But gray whales have displayed an unusual power to regenerate the species, perhaps because they stay relatively close together and so have no difficulty finding each other even when their numbers are small. By the nineteen-twenties, gray whales were again to be found off the California coast. The hunting was resumed, and again the whales were nearly exterminated. In 1938, when there were only a few hundred left, they were protected by an international agreement. In the years since, they have once more recovered remarkably. In recent years, the Russians are known to have resumed the killing during the whales' northern sojourn, in what they claim are moderate numbers.

MIDWAY down the dry, rocky west coast of Baja California, there is a great, shallow lagoon known as Scammon Lagoon, after its discoverer, the same Captain Charles Scammon who described the humpbacks' "amorous antics." In 1857, the Captain had set forth from San Francisco to go whaling and "elephanting" (killing the huge, preposterous-looking, and helpless elephant seals that inhabited the rocks along the coast). Three hundred and fifty miles south of San Diego, off

Sebastián Vizcaíno Bay, he steered his bark past rolling surf and through a narrow channel, and found himself in a vast, tranquil inland lake surrounded by desert and filled with great gray whales. He had discovered the grays' major breeding ground, where, as he reported in his memoirs, they "gathered in large numbers, passing and repassing into and out of the estuaries, or slowly raising their colossal forms midway above the surface, falling over on their sides as if by accident and dashing the water into foam and spray about them."

The Captain sent out his whaleboats, and two large cows were easily killed. But the next morning, as a boat pursued a whale, the whale smashed it with its flukes, spilling the crew in all directions and injuring many of them. A relief boat was staved by another whale. The crew members were so demoralized by these attacks that when next they attempted to harpoon a whale most of them jumped overboard the moment it appeared beside them. One man dove, as he supposed, into the water, but landed on the flukes of the whale. Miraculously, he was not hurt. The Captain found his position peculiar: his vessel safe in smooth water, with countless whales nearby, but the men so panic-stricken that he couldn't man a boat. He had brought along a primitive type of explosive harpoon (or "bomb lance"), which he now decided to try out. With this weapon, his men safely killed all the whales the ship could handle and returned to San Francisco "so deeply laden that her scuppers were washed by the rippling tide."

Scammon's success soon brought other whalers down the coast. He described the scene in the lagoon the next season, when nine vessels and twenty or thirty whaleboats were there:

> The scene of slaughter was exceedingly picturesque and unusually exciting, especially on a calm morning, when the mirage would transform not only the boats and their crews into fantastic imagery, but the whales, as they sent forth their towering spouts of aqueous vapor, frequently tinted with blood, would appear greatly distorted. . . . The boats . . . would be seen gliding over the molten-looking surface of the water, with a . . . colossal form of the whale appearing for an instant, like a spectre . . . while the report of the bomb-guns would sound like the sudden discharge of musketry; but one cannot fully realize, unless he be an eyewitness, the intense and boisterous excitement of the reckless pursuit. . . . Numbers of [boats] will be fast to whales at the same time, and the stricken animals, in their efforts to escape, can be seen darting in every direction through the water, or breaching headlong clear of its surface, coming down with a splash that sends columns of foam in every direction. . . . The men in the boats shout and yell . . . it is one continually changing aquatic battle scene.

During the eighteen-fifties, the hunting of gray whales extended along the coast of upper and lower California. "Every navigable lagoon of the region was discovered and explored, and the animals were hunted in every winding and intricate estuary. . . .

In the seasons of 1858 and 1859, not only the bays and lagoons were teeming [with whalers], but the outside coast was lined with ships, from San Diego southward to Cape St. Lucas," wrote Captain Scammon. The Captain wondered if the killing hadn't been overdone:

The large bays and lagoons, where these animals once congregated, brought forth and nurtured their young, are already nearly deserted. The mammoth bones . . . lie bleaching on the shores of those silvery waters, and are scattered along the broken coasts, from Siberia to the Gulf of California; and ere long it may be questioned whether this mammal will not be numbered among the extinct species of the Pacific.

The Captain's prophecy was twice almost fulfilled, but now there are estimated to be from eight to fourteen thousand gray whales—enough to make them a major tourist attraction. On their migratory journey, hundreds can be seen from the California shore, and people gather at vantage points or go out in small boats to watch them pass. In recent seasons, the San Diego Natural History Museum has chartered a large excursion fishing boat to take people three hundred and fifty miles down the coast to Scammon Lagoon for a closer look, and last year I was among those who made the trip. For two days, our boat—the *HM 85*, eighty-five feet long, with forty of us aboard, including the crew—sailed down the coast, stopping for brief, fascinating shore excursions at the rocky islets of San Benitos and San Martín, which are part of Mexico and are inhabited only by seasonal fishermen, elephant seals, sea lions, and birds. In the evenings, in the crowded cabin, I talked with Dr. William A. Burns, the museum director, about gray whales. Burns is not a biologist, but he is thoroughly acquainted with the subject. He is a former New Yorker—a squarely built man with warm blue eyes, great enthusiasm, and a large repertoire of entertaining stories. In discussing the whales, he gave credit for his information to the museum's whale specialist, Dr. Raymond M. Gilmore, whose title is Research Associate in Marine Mammals, and who has studied the gray whales extensively and made many trips to Scammon.

The California gray whale makes the longest migration of any mammal. The trip from its summer pasture in the northern seas to Baja California covers between four thousand and six thousand miles, depending on the route, and takes about three months of steady swimming. The gray whale cruises at four knots and covers from sixty to eighty nautical miles in twenty-four hours. It does not pause to eat, and probably sleeps little, if at all. Gray whales have been seen pegging along even on the darkest nights. How the whale navigates is not definitely known, but it is believed to use the position of the sun and, since it follows the coast for long stretches (the southward-migrating whales first come near shore in numbers off Oregon), underwater landmarks as well. Dr. Gilmore thinks that it is also guided by the remembered taste of sediment in the water that flows out of lagoons and estuaries.

It appears that this tremendous round trip of anywhere from eight to twelve thousand miles and the two months' stay in the lagoon—which is taken up with the strenuous activities of mating, and, for females, giving birth and producing milk— are fuelled by only four months of feeding in the northern waters in the summer. Most cetologists think the gray whale eats little or nothing on migration or in the lagoon, unless it accidentally runs into suitable small fish or squid. (Dr. Theodore Walker, a former associate at the Scripps Institution of Oceanography, has generated controversy by disputing this. He claims that gray whales shovel up food from the bottom of the lagoons, but Dr. Gilmore points out that every whale slaughtered on migration has had an empty stomach and that northbound whales are thin, or "dry," as the whalers used to call it.) Whether or not the gray whales feed in winter, their feeding habits are unique. In shallow water, they plow up the soft, sandy bottom with their snouts to stir up small invertebrates that they filter out of the water with their baleen.

When the whales start south, they are on a tight schedule. Pregnant females are in the van of the migration, for babies born in the cold, rough water of the open sea might die. Mating, gestation, and birth are all neatly arranged so that they happen in the right place and at the right time. The gestation period is thirteen months. After giving birth, a female spends eleven months nursing and resting. She mates during her next stay in the lagoon and carries the baby through the rich summer months, and it is born in the south the second winter after the previous birth. On the wintering grounds, then, half the mature females are giving birth or nursing and half are mating.

O N our third morning, after an early breakfast, we rounded a buoy at the entrance to Scammon Lagoon. Ahead of us were high white sand dunes. On the right, breakers extended half a mile offshore. I admired Captain Scammon's nerve at taking his bark into these waters, and I wondered if this was where he had seen whales playing in the surf, as he described them in his memoirs:

About the shoals at the mouth of one of the lagoons, in 1860, we saw large numbers of the monsters. It was at the low stage of the tide, and the shoal places were plainly marked by the constantly foaming breakers. To our surprise we saw many of the whales going through the surf where the depth of water was barely sufficient to float them. . . . One in particular, lay for a half hour in the breakers, playing, as seals often do . . . turning from side to side with half-extended fins . . . at times making a playful spring with its bending flukes, throwing its body clear of the water, coming down with a heavy splash . . . with the heavy swell the animal would roll over in a listless manner, to all appearance enjoying the sport intensely.

I wished that I could witness intense enjoyment in a whale, but our captain did not take us close to the breakers. As we entered the channel, the dark-green seas became violently choppy and we were warned by the crew to hang on tight. Black-backed gulls flapped along beside us. Then I saw ahead a white plume rise from the surface of the water, hang, and vanish. Shortly after that, we overtook a whale surging along, its broad back awash and gleaming; it was heading purposefully for the entrance to the lagoon, as we were. Ten minutes later, we were out of the chop and inside the lagoon. There was sudden calm. On one side of us were sculptured mountains of white sand; on the other, rippling water reached to the horizon. The main lagoon is a long, irregular crescent varying from five to ten miles in width and extending into the desert for almost thirty miles. There are many shallows, islands, and sand flats. Here and there, smaller tributary lagoons branch off. All around is one of the world's most desolate deserts—the Vizcaíno, which matches the Sahara for dryness. There is only one natural source of fresh water within hundreds of square miles—Ojo de Liebre, or Jack Rabbit Spring, where there was once a small settlement. The shores surrounding us were roadless and totally uninhabited.

A rusty fishing boat, at anchor, now came into view. It was serving as a base ship for outboard-engine skiffs we would use for following whales in the lagoon. We anchored. The skiffs were brought alongside, and the tourists, wearing orange life jackets, climbed into them. I found a seat beside Dr. Burns. The sailor at the tiller of our boat steered us toward the center of the lagoon, where several whales had spouted, and we buzzed over the water. I regretted the motor, for I would rather have drifted and waited for whales to appear, but Dr. Burns explained that chasing the whales in this fashion gave the tourists a better chance of getting pictures, and that was what most of them wanted.

Within five minutes, we were coming up on a whale. First, its head appeared. I saw the long slit of its mouth, the small eyes, and a pattern of barnacles. It exhaled, with a sound like a steam pants presser, and then its huge back rolled out, ridged toward the tail with a series of small knobs, like the back of a prehistoric beast. We were so close that I felt my heart lurch. Being on the same level with a whale was quite different from viewing one from the deck of a big boat. The whale rose, blew, sank, rose again, blew another sighing, steamy breath, and disappeared with a wave of its flukes, leaving a swirling slick on the surface. The flukes, Dr. Burns said, are about ten feet across, weigh several hundred pounds, and can deliver a blow like that of a rubber sledgehammer. A couple of years ago, a diver swimming off La Jolla met a whale underwater and made the mistake of touching its tail as it glided by. The startled whale gave a mighty swish of its flukes, grazing the diver and knocking his mask off while the barnacles on its skin cut a gash in his forehead. He was lucky to survive. The flukes are a formidable means of defense for the whale, and Captain Scammon reported that sometimes angry mother whales also overturned boats

by "rooting" them with their snouts, like pigs over-
turning a trough.

For the next hour, we motored here and there,
seeing whales now close, now far off. Dr. Burns
said he had heard it estimated that there were two
or three thousand of them within the lagoon at this
time. (Meanwhile, other groups of grays were
wintering in other lagoons.) Every minute or so, a
spout rose somewhere. We often saw whales performing what are called "spy hops"—sticking their
heads eight or ten feet out of the water and hanging
there for a few seconds, apparently intent on seeing
what is going on. The most startling displays were
the whales' extraordinary breaches, usually per-
formed by the males. A forty-foot whale on end
towers as high as a three-story building. This incredible length shoots out of the water at terrific
speed, hangs in the air, and falls amid fountains of
spray. The whales may breach out of sheer exuber-
ance, or the breaching may be primarily a display
of strength by males, or possibly slapping against
the water allays an itch from barnacles; occasionally mothers and calves also breach.

A number of times, we came upon mothers and
young swimming side by side, the baby whale
rising and falling in a rhythm that exactly matched
that of its parent. These calves were a few weeks
old. A newborn gray is from twelve to seventeen
feet long and weighs from fifteen hundred to three
thousand pounds. Captain Scammon wrote that as
birth time arrived the pregnant whales collected in
the remote reaches of the lagoon and "huddled

together so thickly that it was difficult for a boat to cross the waters without coming in contact with them." He also wrote of the whales' strong maternal feelings: "This species of whale manifests the greatest affection for its young, and seeks the sheltered estuaries lying under a tropical sun, as if to warm its offspring." He described how a whale struck with a harpoon would attempt to escape by running along the bottom, and noted that if a mother was harpooned and lost sight of her calf she would instantly "stop and 'sweep' around in search." He added, "If the boat comes in contact with her, it is quite sure to be staved." In the case of the wounding of a calf, he wrote, "the parent animal, in her frenzy, will chase the boats, and . . . overturn them with her head, or dash them in pieces with a stroke of her ponderous flukes." Whalers sometimes deliberately shot a calf and towed it into shallow water because the mother would follow and could be more easily killed there.

We came across several sleeping whales, lying awash like logs. Having slept so little on migration, the gray whales catch up in the lagoons. We saw a sleeping mother whose calf was apparently trying to wake her by splashing and nudging as we approached. She seemed to wake with a start, and both of them dived out of sight.

What caused the greatest sensation in our skiff was coming across whales courting. This activity often involves not two animals but a trio. Since half the females are pregnant or nursing, only half are in breeding condition, so there are two males to every available female. The exact role of the second male—whether he is a bystander or a participant, perhaps assisting by lying across the female to stabilize her—is debated by cetologists. Whatever is happening, the three of them make a tremendous flurry in the water, rising, falling, splashing, and revolving, with giant flippers waving above the surface. We came on several such scenes, but nothing was explicit until, quite close to our boat, a whale revolved in the water, turning belly up on the surface, and there was a brief but distinct glimpse of its long, pink, erect penis. Our boatload was divided between the happy photographers who had caught this memorable view and the chagrined photographers who had missed it. Dr. Burns was jubilant, since both winners and losers had had a fair chance, and the trip was now undeniably a success.

When we got back to the *HM 85*, two people who were living aboard the rusty anchored fishing boat had come over to visit. They were Peter Paul Ott, a wildlife painter and photographer from Laguna Beach, and his wife, Holly. They had been living on the boat for two months, and had found the beauty and the solitude marvellous. Ott described some of their experiences with whales. He said that when the boat was quiet, with the auxiliary engine for generating electricity turned off, the whales seemed to become curious, and made closer and closer passes. One evening after dark, he had heard a whale blow very close. A large baby whale and a huge mother were coming straight for the boat. Ott shone a light on them and saw the calf dive underneath, looking like a blimp outlined in phosphorescence. The calf emerged, rolled over on its side, and looked up at Ott with its ridiculously small eye. Ott tried to scratch its back, but couldn't reach it. He said that sleeping whales sometimes collided with the boat as they drifted with the tide, hitting with a dull thud. In the calm of the night, a whale's blow could be heard for miles, and a breach sounded like a cannon as it echoed among the dunes.

Ott's most distressing experience, he said, was with an orphaned and injured calf. He saw it swimming alone, listing to one side. It became stranded on a beach. With an oar, Ott was able to heave it back in the water. There were two large whales nearby, but they offered no help. The next day, the orphan was stranded again, higher on the beach, and there was nothing that Ott could do for it. It rolled its eyes, watching him, and winced as he touched it. Its skin was so delicate that it broke at the touch of a fingernail. Gulls settled on it and tore it. The whale waved its tail as the gulls pecked, but it made no cry. Ott concealed himself and watched. Coyotes came and circled. It was very gruesome, Ott said, and he could think of no way to help or to administer a coup de grâce. He was greatly relieved when the whale died.

Ott and his wife had explored some of the shore and found tremendous salt marshes, with thousands of birds, and an island that held twenty-five or thirty pair of nesting ospreys—an extraordinary concentration of these increasingly rare birds. On the way back from an excursion in their fourteen-foot skiff, they accidentally ran into the midst of a pod of six whales, several within arm's reach of the boat at once. They found the moment both wonderful and terrifying; an accidental flip of a fluke could have overturned them and drowned the motor. Ott was well aware that the water teems with sharks. He had just caught a leopard shark twelve feet long.

When I woke the next morning, a soft gray haze hung over the lagoon, and the water was like a dark mirror. The whales seemed to be moving more slowly or resting with their whole length on the surface. The *HM 85* coasted deeper into the lagoon, across shallows where weeds grew. I went ashore with a small group and walked alone on a beach bordered by strange rocks and twisted, thorny desert shrubs. The solitude seemed boundless; Captain Scammon and his bomb lances and cooking pots had left no trace. It was perhaps the most beautiful meeting place of land and sea that I had ever seen. Once in a while, as I walked along the silent, endless beach, a whale would rise just off-shore, and I would hear its soft, sighing breath. It was a companionable sound.

IN the nineteen-fifties, Dr. Paul Dudley White, the heart specialist, in the course of attempts to measure the heartbeat of a gray whale, pursued several in Scammon Lagoon, trying to implant a harpoon carrying electrocardiographic equipment.

After various difficulties, he at last connected with a whale, but the resulting data were far from clear, and he gave up. In 1965, Dr. Robert Elsner, a physiologist from the Scripps Institution, and Dr. David Kenney, a veterinarian who was also a vice-president of a marine park in San Diego called Sea World, decided to try their luck. They hired a Japanese whale gunner and went to Scammon, where they harpooned a baby whale and lifted it to the deck in a net. When the heart recordings were finished, it seemed useless to put the little whale back in the water, since it could only die of its wound, so they lashed it to the deck of their boat and took it back to San Diego. The trip lasted three days, but the whale lived, and was put in a pool at Sea World. Dr. Kenney patched it up, and, in spite of a collapsed lung, the whale amazed its captors by surviving for almost two months.

This episode convinced Kenney that, with gentle handling, a baby whale could be captured and kept indefinitely. He was fascinated by the possibility of raising such animals in captivity, and the other Sea World directors agreed to the project. In March, 1971, Kenney again went to Scammon Lagoon. After a number of chases in a small boat, he maneuvered a mother and her calf under the bow of the boat, slipped a noose around the calf, and hauled it to the beach. The mother left as darkness fell. In the morning, the calf was worked onto a stretcher and floated out to a larger vessel, where it was put in a converted fish well for the trip to San Diego. The calf, an eighteen-foot female, arrived in good health and was put in a large, round tank. She was weighed in a sling and tipped the scale at forty-three hundred pounds. Now Dr. Kenney tried to fabricate whale milk from its known ingredients. The resulting mixture had the consistency of cooling fudge and would not go through a feeding tube, so he improvised a concoction of heavy cream, ground squid and fish, cod-liver oil, yeast, vitamins, and water. The whale, who had been named Gigi, reluctantly partook of it. Kenney's laboratory-animal manager, a tall, kindly Nebraskan named Bud N. Donahoo, was in charge of the feedings, for which the water in the whale's tank was lowered. To get the tube into Gigi's esophagus, Donahoo had to thrust his arm into her mouth, parting the bristles of baleen that hung like curtains from her jaw. This was apparently somewhat painful at first, but after a while there was a permanent gap and no further pain. In her first two weeks in the tank, Gigi lost a hundred and fifty pounds. Then she began to gain and grow, at the rate of twenty-seven pounds and a third of an inch a day. She was moved to a larger tank. The only abnormal thing about Gigi was that she seemed exceptionally fond of sleeping, even for an infant. A dolphin was put in with her for company, and girl swimmers from Sea World's corps of performing Sea Maids were employed to swim beside her, poking at her to keep her awake. After a while, Gigi came to life and began to tear around the tank, jumping, flopping, rolling, and waving her flippers like a normal whale.

An important factor in the successful captivity of Gigi was the relationship that developed between her and Donahoo. He thought of her as a lonely, confused being, imprisoned in her great sensitive bulk of flesh and isolated by lack of communication. He also realized that she was only a baby and must long for reassurance. He searched for some way to make contact with her. By accident, when he was cleaning the tank one day, he sprayed a hose on her flukes, and she lifted them to hold them in the spray. It was a clue that she might enjoy being rubbed. He began touching her gently. At first, she shuddered and twitched, but soon he was rubbing her from nose to tail, and she relaxed under his hands. His next problem was to find a means of communication. He talked to her constantly, but it didn't seem likely that she would understand words, so he decided on a system of pats as signals —one pat for attention, two pats to open her mouth, three firm pats for "No" or "Be quiet." The whale learned these commands. Now Donahoo was able to move her about in the tank, and this was a tremendous help in handling her. With the water lowered, he could stand by her head, signalling to her, and she would wiggle her great bulk to follow him.

Gigi's weaning took place when Donahoo felt her sucking on his hand while he was putting the tube in her throat. He put a squid in her mouth, and she swallowed it gratefully. Soon she was eating squid by the handful, and then sucking them up from the floor of her tank. This was a development that fascinated scientific observers, for never before had the mechanics of a gray whale eating been directly observed. The cetologist William E. Schevill, of Harvard, watched as she scooped in the squid—turning on her side, opening one side of her mouth and sucking like a giant vacuum cleaner, and then ramming her tongue forward to squirt out the water. Once weaned, Gigi learned to take food from the hands of people swimming beside her or to come to the side of the tank at the sight of a bucket. When Donahoo dropped the water level and approached her, she would come over to him eagerly, with her mouth open.

One of the things that greatly puzzled Donahoo was how Gigi could distinguish him from anyone else. When other handlers tried to do things with her—often in connection with the numerous scientific tests she was undergoing—she often raised such a ruckus that they were forced to stop and send for Donahoo. As soon as he arrived, no matter what he was wearing—and in a wet-suit identity is well hidden—Gigi calmed down. Donahoo never figured out how Gigi recognized him, but it seemed clear that he had become her parental figure. Mutual affection also sprang up between the whale and one of the Sea Maids, a girl named Sue Bailey, who was deft at feeding Gigi.

By the end of Gigi's first year in the tank at Sea World, she had grown to nearly seven tons and was twenty-seven feet long. Scientists from numerous institutions had made a great variety of physiological tests, and Dr. Kenney had filing cabinets full of new whale data. Her rate of growth, food consumption, blood composition, and respiratory function had been recorded. But, to Dr. Kenney's regret, the managers of Sea World, which by now was spending two hundred dollars a day just on her food, felt that the upkeep expense was prohibitive, and they decided that soon they would have to put her back in the sea, before she got too big to be moved. When I heard about this, and having visited Gigi's birthplace at Scammon Lagoon, I decided to go to Sea World to see her.

At the gate of the park, I was met by Bud Donahoo, a tall, athletic-looking man in his late thirties with kind blue eyes and a boyish face, and Sue Bailey, a pretty girl with long brown hair. They led me to a circular tank, fifty feet across. A huge gray cylinder rested at the bottom of the tank. "That's her favorite place—by the water inlet," Sue said. After a minute or two, Gigi slowly pumped her flukes, rose, and began to glide majestically in a slow circle on the surface, blowing leisurely spouts. I said I thought she was lovely, and Donahoo and Sue beamed. Gigi sank peacefully to the bottom and went to sleep.

I went back the next morning, at the suggestion of Donahoo, who had told me that the water in the tank would be lowered then and Sue would attempt to ride her. First, Sue, in a wet-suit, approached the whale, splashing water ahead of her as though to announce her coming. She splashed Gigi's head, and then put her hands on her back and rubbed her vigorously. Donahoo, carrying a bucket of squid, approached and also patted her. "She's talking!" he shouted up at me. "Can you hear it?" Water splashing loudly over the rim of an adjoining tank drowned out any sound from the whale, but, as I watched, her whole body swelled and heaved in response to Donahoo's caress. Her huge, rubbery person seemed to emanate feeling. Sue took a handful of squid and began stuffing them into Gigi's mouth, her arm disappearing to the elbow. As Donahoo and Sue went on rubbing and patting vigorously, and stuffing in squid, the huge cylinder of flesh vibrated with responsive animation.

Then Sue put her hands on Gigi's back and leaped astride. Gigi's tail fluttered, and, ponderously she began to move. As they slowly circled the tank, Donahoo climbed out and joined me. "If Gigi didn't like being ridden, she'd roll Sue off any time she liked," he said. The whale and the girl went around and around, Sue sitting astride her like a mahout aboard an elephant, and the whale's flukes pumping rhythmically. Then Gigi came to a halt. Sue patted her head and she moved again. Donahoo said that she was responding to signals from Sue. Sue stopped her, dismounted, and resumed caressing Gigi around the head and stuffing her mouth with squid.

Donahoo said it amazed him how Gigi could discriminate between different kinds of food. Given twenty pounds of squid with a few mackerel mixed in, she would swallow the squid and spit out the mackerel. "She's usually a docile animal," he said.

"But she can be aggressive. She bobs her head up and down and shakes her whole body from side to side when she's perturbed. She's knocked me across the tank many times. But I can always calm her down. The signal to be quiet is three firm pats. She may start right up again, but then I quiet her again until she gets over whatever it is that's disturbing her." Next, Donahoo told me about talking to the whale. He said Gigi made deep interior noises that he couldn't describe. One day, early in their relationship, he tapped out a peculiar rhythm on her head and was astonished to hear the whale repeat the sequence. He tried another rhythm, and she repeated that, too. He concluded that Gigi was trying to talk to him. Thereafter, throughout her babyhood, he had daily conversations with her, tapping and getting answers. Now her answers had tapered off, perhaps in discouragement at getting no whale sounds back, but she still talked on occasion. "I believe that this animal can be communicated with by sound," Donahoo said. To his regret, none of the visiting scientists had been interested in the phenomenon, because they did not regard it as part of the whale's natural behavior. Donahoo told me that he had learned to distinguish at least four different sounds made by Gigi. When she uttered them, he said, the whole tank vibrated. "The vibrations hit your legs," he continued. "When she's happy, there's one big grunt. Her whole body swells up. Sometimes she makes other sounds before or after, but the happy sound is just one."

Sue had mounted again, and she and Gigi were

again making stately circles. Then the whale gave a leisurely roll and Sue fell off. She remounted and was dumped again. Leaving Gigi, she climbed the ladder and joined us.

PLANS for releasing Gigi were made by Dr. William Evans, a marine biologist at the Naval Undersea Center, in San Diego, who had been studying her. He felt that she would have the best chance of survival if she was released in spring, when the gray whales were migrating north to the feeding grounds. Even so, he suspected that release would be a shock to her; the sudden change to the darkness of the sea's depths, the noise of ships' propellers, and the need to find food would be "harrowing," he told a newspaper reporter. He worked out a way to attach an instrument package, which could store and transmit data, to her back, in order to keep track of her after her release. A few weeks ahead of time, large stitches of nylon thread were sewn through the blubber of her back, with loops sticking up to hold the equipment.

Before dawn on a cool March day, Gigi was wrapped in a sling and hoisted from the tank by a crane. She was put down on a sixteen-inch-thick foam-rubber mattress on a thirty-two-foot Navy flatbed truck and covered with wet blankets. Donahoo and Sue rode with her, patting and reassuring her. She breathed quickly, indicating apprehension, but gave no signs of serious distress. The truck drove six miles through dark city streets to a Navy pier, and there Gigi was transferred to a barge, which carried her four and a half miles out to sea. Then, a few minutes before ten, a crane lowered the sling into the water. As it touched the surface, Donahoo dived over the side and, when the sling was released, pulled the canvas clear. The whale gave a graceful wave of her flukes and swam free. Donahoo swam beside her for twenty or thirty yards, and then she dived. She surfaced two or three hundred yards away, made a wide sweep around the boat, as though orienting herself, and started north. There were other northbound whales in the area, and their spouts were visible a half mile away. For several days, Evans tracked her in a small research vessel, picking up signals from the transmitter on her back. This was more difficult than he had expected. The transmitter sent its signals by means of a two-foot-tall antenna, which operated only when it was out of water. Evans had failed to allow for the fact that yearling whales do not roll as far out of the water as adults do, and so the signals were relatively brief and infrequent. When Evans left Gigi, a Navy plane picked up her signal, and her northward progress was recorded. She covered eighty miles in the first four days. The instruments indicated that she was diving to maximum depths of two and three hundred feet. From the plane, observers saw signs in the water that she had found something to eat. At one point, to Evans' dismay, she lingered to play in a kelp bed and bent the antenna, reducing the range of the signals from twenty-five or thirty miles to five or ten. Nevertheless, her progress was followed by plane for more than two weeks longer. At that point, the funds allotted for the project were exhausted and the Navy ceased to follow her. And at the last report, early in May, she was with other gray whales north of Monterey. She had covered more than five hundred miles. The transmitter was designed to work for nine months, and there was a remote hope that a ship or plane would pick up her signals during the summer or on her return journey south, but this didn't occur.

In any event, for the first time in all the eons of human and whale existence a great whale had been in the power of human beings and had escaped with its life.